VISION IN WORSHIP

By the same author
Festal Drama in Deutero-Isaiah

VISION IN WORSHIP

*The Relation of Prophecy and
Liturgy in the Old Testament*

J. H. Eaton

London   SPCK

First published 1981
SPCK
Holy Trinity Church
Marylebone Road
London NW1 4DU

Typeset by Computacomp (UK) Ltd
Fort William, Scotland
Printed in Great Britain by
Lowe & Brydone Printers Ltd
Thetford, Norfolk

ISBN 0 281 03800 7

To my dear sister Muriel

Contents

Abbreviations

BDB	Brown, Driver, Briggs: *Oxford Hebrew Lexicon*, 1906
BHS	*Biblia Hebraica Stuttgartensia*
CPAI	Johnson: *The Cultic Prophet in Ancient Israel*
CPIP	Johnson: *The Cultic Prophet and Israel's Psalmody*
FDDI	Eaton: *Festal Drama in Deutero-Isaiah*
G	Greek Version (LXX)
JTS	*Journal of Theological Studies*
KP	Eaton: *Kingship and the Psalms*
M	Massoretic Hebrew Text
ONHZ	Eaton: *Obadiah, Nahum, Habakkuk, Zephaniah*
RBH	Eaton (ed.): *Readings in Biblical Hebrew*, 2 vols.
S	Syriac Version
SKAI	Johnson: *Sacral Kingship in Ancient Israel*
T	Targum
TI	*Tradition and Interpretation*, see Eaton: 'The Psalms and Israelite Worship'
V	Vulgate
ZAW	*Zeitschrift für die alttestamentliche Wissenschaft*

Preface

I have cited modern works in brief form, usually with the author's name only; the details appear in the lists of abbreviations and works cited. For biblical references where Hebrew and English numbers differ, I have placed the English after an oblique stroke.

I have not been alone in feeling for many years that the prophetic books of the Hebrew Bible are usually presented in the classroom in a way that obscures and even distorts their relation to Israel's worship. It seemed to me that a major step towards a comprehensive reassessment of these prophets would be to let the numerous passages of plainly liturgical character speak for themselves and alongside comparable materials from the psalms. I was much encouraged to take this step by invitations to lecture in two keen and stimulating gatherings, the Vacation Term for Biblical Study (at St Anne's College, Oxford, August 1977) and the Irish Biblical Association (at Bellinter, near Navan, April 1979), and I am indebted to them for their encouraging reception of various parts of the present work.

In the nature of the case, it seemed right to cite many of these passages generously and in a fresh translation. I hope to have mediated these ancient voices to make their own fascinating and often awe-inspiring impression.

Department of Theology   JOHN EATON
University of Birmingham

Introduction

My aim is to examine the contribution of prophetic ministries to the great occasions of Israelite worship. Such an examination should throw new light both on the nature of prophecy and on the nature of that worship.

My method will be to use the psalms to depict four elements of worship relevant to prophecy, and in each case then to adduce material from the prophetic books where prophets seem to be contributing to just such elements. The four elements will be:

1. God's advent with power and visionary effects
2. His great speeches to his covenanted people
3. His dialogues and disputes with his people
4. His oracles for the royal rites.

I believe we shall here be exploiting some very rich biblical mineral fields, which were discovered over fifty years ago, and have since been quite well surveyed, but for one reason or another then little exploited.

Early in this century, Gunkel's[1] researches into literary types and forms showed clearly the presence of prophetic material in the psalms, and also the presence of psalmic or liturgical forms in the prophets. Mowinckel[2] made a decisive contribution in treating this prophetic material in the psalms as belonging to actual procedures of worship, the speech of God being conveyed to worshippers by inspired ministers. A. R. Johnson[3] collected the evidence from the Old Testament to show the importance of prophetic ministries at the sanctuaries, and he has recently expounded psalms which he regards as utterances of cultic prophets. There have been fruitful contributions at particular points by, for example, E. Würthwein, Graf Reventlow, and von Waldow. But, in general, modern scholars have been inclined to let the trail grow cold. So enduring has been the nineteenth-century tradition that great prophecy must come from outside the institutions of worship, that the full force of the evidence has

1

generally been warded off. It is timely, then, to bring together the evidence of the psalms and prophets in the manner I have proposed and to see what it will do to our understanding of worship and of prophecy.

1 God's Advent in Victory and Salvation

The festal advent in the psalms

Since Mowinckel showed the dynamic and dramatic character of the Israelite festivals in his studies of 1921–4, there has been much debate as to what texts belong to this experience and exactly how it should be understood. However, there is now wide agreement that the main themes and moods of the hymns do take us to the heart of pre-exilic worship and in particular to the autumn festival[1] at Jerusalem. It is clear enough that the worshippers at that festival experienced the deity as active, coming among them with power, demonstrating his sovereignty over all.

How prominent this experience was in the festivals can be judged from the reactions of awe and jubilation which are amply attested in the psalms. The combination of God's dramatic presence and the consequent excitement is well illustrated from Psalm 47:

> All peoples, clap your hands,
> acclaim God with jubilant cries!
> For Yahweh is manifest as the Most High inspiring awe,[2]
> the supreme King over all the earth....

> God has ascended with acclamation,
> Yahweh with the noise of horns.
> Play and sing to God, play and sing,
> play and sing to our King, play and sing!
> To the King indeed of all the world,
> to God triumphant[3] play and sing!
> God has become King over the nations.
> God now sits on his holy throne.

The same sense of excitement at God's dramatic presence runs through Psalm 96:

> Sing to Yahweh a new song,
> sing to Yahweh, all the earth,
> bear tidings of his salvation from day to day,
> tell of his glory among the nations,
> among the peoples tell his wonders!

For great is Yahweh and very glorious,
manifest in dread power over all the gods....

Splendour and majesty shine before him,
glory and beauty are in his sanctuary.
Attribute to Yahweh, clans of the peoples,
attribute to Yahweh all glory and power,
attribute to Yahweh the glory of his name,
bear gifts and enter his courts,
fall down before Yahweh in his divine majesty!
Dance because of him, all the world,
declare among the nations, Yahweh reigns!
So the world is secured and will not totter,
he rules the peoples with justice.

Let heaven make merry and earth rejoice,
let the sea thunder and all that lives in it,
the fields exult and all that is in them,
let trees sing out, all the trees of the forest,
before Yahweh, for he has entered,
he has come to rule the earth.
He rules the world with right order,
the peoples in his faithfulness.

A similar response to the manifest Yahweh can be illustrated
from Psalm 149:

Sing to Yahweh a new song,
his praise in the assembly of the covenanters.
Let Israel rejoice at his Creator,
the children of Zion be merry over their King,
let them praise his name with circling dances,
sing and play to him with hand-drums and harps!
For Yahweh accepts his people,
he has adorned the afflicted with robes of salvation.

The significance of the ecstatic music, the singing, dancing,
clapping, and cheering is further illustrated by Psalm 68, which
also explains the phrase in Psalm 96, 'he has entered, he has
come'. For in Psalm 68 a great procession winds into the
sanctuary, representing the ascent of God to his throne,
triumphant over all evil, ready to rule the world with goodness.
The presence of God is symbolized in the procession, probably by
the ark, and all around are the musicians and dancers:

Let God arise and his enemies be scattered
and his foes flee before him!
Like the driving of smoke, so drive them away,
like the melting of wax at the fire,
so perish the wicked at the presence of God!
But let the true-hearted make merry,
exult before God and rejoice with glad noise!
Sing to God, sing and play to his name,
prepare the way for him who rides the clouds,[4]
with chanting of his name Yah exult before him....

They see your procession, O God,
the procession of my God and King into the sanctuary.
First go the singers, at the rear the harpers,
in the middle the girls playing hand-drums.

From such lengthy and descriptive texts we are then able to understand such a compact piece as Psalm 150, where only the reaction of jubilation is expressed. It would be foolish to think such ecstasy of joy was conjured out of the air. Rather it is again the reaction to the divine action in worship; God's presence has been dramatically signified. The cymbals accompany the $t^e r \bar{u}\,' \bar{a}$ (v. 6/5), acclamation of the God manifest in royal triumph. He has taken his throne in his temple, symbolic of his reign over the firmament. Temple and heaven are one, and one are the praises in heaven and earth:

Praise Yah!
Praise God in his sanctuary,
praise him in his glorious firmament,
praise him with telling of his mighty deeds,
praise him according to the greatness of his power,
praise him with blast of horns,
praise him with lutes and harps,
praise him with hand-drums and circling dance,
praise him with strings and flutes,
praise him with the cymbals for proclamation,
praise him with the cymbals for acclamation!
All that breathes, praise Yah!
Praise Yah!

From texts such as these, then, it is apparent that the festal joy was intended as response to the dramatically signified coming or revelation of God. At the time and in the manner of his appointing, he came in symbol and sacrament and made new for

5

his worshippers his work of salvation, upholding the order of life
and goodness. His omnipotence, pictured as kingship, was thus
represented in a kind of drama. The relation of the eternal ideal
and the imperfect 'today' became in the ritual context a matter of
events or acts. With use of processions and other symbolic
movements, there was enacted a sacrament of the defeat of evil,
the commencement of God's perfect reign, the healing of the
afflicted. The glad news that Yahweh now reigns is received with
prostration, applause, dancing and rapturous music.

Already we may feel it was not arbitrary of the Books of
Chronicles to describe the psalmists as 'seers' (1 Chron. 25.5;
2 Chron. 29.30; 35.15) and their work as 'prophesying' (1 Chron.
25.1–3; cf. Exod. 15.20). Indeed, texts such as I have adduced
have affinity with prophecy in several respects. For here are
words which depict the appearing of God and tell of his will and
power. The depiction has visionary quality, as may be illustrated
from Psalm 93:

Yahweh now reigns!
He has robed himself in majesty,
Yahweh has robed himself, has girded himself
in glory.

Likewise from Psalm 104:

Yahweh my God,
you show yourself very great,
with splendour and majesty you have robed yourself,
you are wrapped in light as in a garment.

Or again, from Psalm 50:

God of gods, Yahweh, speaks
and summons the world
from the rising of the sun to its setting.
From Zion, perfection of beauty,
God gives his radiance.
Our God has come and is not silent.
Fire consumes before him
and around him tempest rages.

What visionary power fills the portrayal of God's appearing in
Psalm 97!

Yahweh now reigns!
Let the earth rejoice,

let the many coastlands be merry!
Clouds and darkness are around him,
right and justice form the dais for his throne,
fire goes before him and licks up his foes round about,
his lightnings light up the world,
the earth sees and dances,
the mountains melt like wax at the presence of Yahweh,
at the presence of the Lord of all the earth,
the heavens tell his righteousness
and all peoples see his glory ...
all gods fall down before him.

The God who so comes to his sanctuary is vividly seen as victor. He has conquered chaos in all its manifold aspects. So the visionary gifts of these psalmists are brought to bear on the warfare of God, which will have been represented in symbolic actions and processions as the background to his ascension to his temple. Against the chaos as waters or water-monster he was imagined to utter a terrifying thunder-roar (Pss. 18; 29; 68; 104; cf. 46; 76); he shoots arrows of lightning and hurls hail and fiery coals (18; 77); he splits the water-foe in two, breaks the dragon's many heads, kills water-courses by drying them up (18; 74; 77; 89). The chaos-foes are sometimes seen rather in the form of nations, their kings and cities. Such who pit themselves against Yahweh, he mows down in heaps (110) or throws them into a faint of terror at his appearing (48; 76). His stunning thunder-word may become an oracle, still a deadly weapon (2; 110). Fortifications and armaments are seen in ruins and burnt heaps across the earth (9; 46; 76). Sometimes God's warfare is envisaged in yet more military form. He is surrounded by thousands upon thousands of chariots (68). His king and his covenanted host are to fight with him; captives are to be taken and prescribed judgements executed upon them (2; 110; 149).

In a variety of briefer references also, vivid portrayal is given. God is seen to be active: he laughs on his throne (Ps. 2.4), he looks down with searching eyes upon mankind (11.4), he holds a sceptre of righteousness in his hand (48.11/10), he lifts a cup brimming with red liquor − judgement for the wicked to drain (75.9/8), he takes his position at the head of the divine council (82.1).

Kinship with prophecy can also be found in the symbolic

7

actions which the psalms imply. It is likely that Yahweh's defeat of evil in his festal appearing was shown forth by such gestures as are common in the prophetic books, as when Jeremiah smashed a pot representing the doomed city (Jer. 19), or Ezekiel modelled the siege of the city with brick, iron plate, etc. (Ezek. 4) and cut off his hair to burn, scatter, etc. in imitation of the future fate of the inhabitants (Ezek. 5). There are certainly strong hints in the similes of Psalm 2.9 and Psalm 68.3/2: foes smashed like earthenware jars or figurines or dispersed like melted wax and driven smoke; and 73.17f. shows how attendance at the sanctuary could strengthen one's confidence in the downfall of the wicked. Certainly the processions were symbolic demonstrations of Yahweh's triumph (Pss. 24 and 68). The sacramental nature of such rites seems to be expressed succinctly in Psalm 48.9f./8f. After depicting the onslaught of the enemy kings on Zion and their annihilation by the epiphany of Yahweh, the psalm continues:

> Just as we heard [i.e. by recital of tradition],
> so we have seen for ourselves
> in the city of Yahweh of Hosts, the city of our God.
> God has established her for ever.
> We have represented ['modelled'][5] your fidelity, O God,
> in the heart of your temple.

As A. R. Johnson noted in his *Cultic Prophet in Ancient Israel* (pp. 42–3), such dramatic worship is akin to the prophetic practice of symbolic acts.

Of course, the processions and other rites expressing Yahweh's salvation and judgement would be subject to his guidance through omen or oracle. One account of such a procession, when David brought the ark to Jerusalem, actually includes an incident which betokened Yahweh's displeasure and caused a long postponement in the completion of the procession (2 Sam. 6). A psalm has been preserved, Psalm 132, which seems to show that David's bringing in of the ark was regularly re-enacted in the autumn festival. It reveals a certain apprehension about the awesome nature of the task and pleads for Yahweh's favour on the strength of his original acceptance of David. The procession can go forward only when the ancient oracle to David is given afresh (v. 11f.), affirming his favour to king and people. We may be sure that in all such ceremonies evidence would be sought that

Yahweh was thus favourably disposed – in the phrase of Psalm 149.4, that 'he accepts his people'. Prophetic ministers must have served in mediating such decisions of God to set the ceremonies in motion and authorize the proclamations. Psalm 85 may illustrate such prophetic service. After the plea to God ending

> Yahweh, show us your fidelity
> and give us your salvation!

come words full of suspense (v. 9/8f.):

> I will listen for what the God Yahweh will speak.

Relief follows with the authorization:

> Yes, he pronounces prosperity for his people, his covenanters,
> though they must not turn back to folly.
> Surely his salvation has drawn near for his worshippers
> that glory may reside in our land....
> The angel of right marches before him,
> his footfall preparing a way.

The assistance of oracular messengers in the festal procession may be indicated in Psalm 68. If the procession came to Zion with the gospel of Yahweh's victory and salvation, it could do so only at Yahweh's command. So we read in verse 12/11:

> The Lord gave the word,
> great was the company of the preachers.

Or, if we may leave that venerable translation:

> The Lord has given the word,
> the bearers of good tidings are a mighty throng.

Thus the Lord sent his oracle of salvation, and the prophetic ministers received it and passed it on as a gospel which all the singers and dancers would publish further. This seems to me to be the situation behind the mysterious opening of the cycle Isaiah 40—55.[6] The exilic prophets draw on the old cultic tradition. A series of voices passes on to other ministers the commission to declare God's favour and to hasten and announce his grand procession of triumph and salvation into Zion:

9

Comfort, comfort my people, says your God,
Speak tenderly to Jerusalem and proclaim to her
that her warfare is accomplished,
her iniquity pardoned!

The voice of one proclaiming:
Clear in the wilderness the way of Yahweh,
level in the desert the highway for our God,
for the mouth of Yahweh commands it!

A voice is saying: Proclaim now!
And they say: What shall I proclaim?
[Cry that] the creature fades like grass ...
but the word of our God endures for ever.

Climb a high mountain, you who carry tidings to Zion,[7]
shout with all your might, you who carry tidings to Jerusalem!
Declare to the cities of Judah, Here comes your God!
See, the Lord Yahweh comes as a champion
and his arm rules in triumph ...
as a shepherd he feeds his flock!

This remarkable passage thus seems to fill out what we see in the psalms of ministers who gave authority to the festal entry of Yahweh as victor and saviour: 'The Lord has given the word, the bearers of good tidings are a mighty throng ... they see your procession, O God, the procession of my God and King into the sanctuary.'

So far, then, we have seen that Israel's festivals formed a fertile setting for some prophetic ministries. There was a vivid sense of God's advent in the gathering, the psalmists depicting his presence with visionary power. Symbolic acts manifested his power over all rivals, his defeat of evil, his faithful care of his people. Messages and portents from God indicated whether he absolved and accepted his people and would indeed enter as Saviour. In all this prophets could make a large contribution, specialists as they were in ecstasy and vision, symbolic acts, and mediation of God's will. What we must now do is to see whether the corpus of prophetic books in fact gives us any examples of prophets mediating visions of Yahweh's advent in connection with worship.

Visions of God's advent and warfare in the prophets

We may begin with the psalm-like poem in Habakkuk 3.[8] It happens to be furnished with annotations like the psalms. There is a heading:

Intercessory psalm,[9] of Habakkuk the prophet [to be rendered as] in lamentation rites.[10]

Then at three places we have *selā*, that mysterious rubric which occurs seventy-one times in the psalms and may be a signal for the congregation to make obeisance. At the end occur two other directions typical of psalms: '[in the manner of psalms] to seek God's favour'(?), and 'with stringed instruments'.

These annotations suggest that the piece was at some stage used in the same way as the psalms, and that in origin the work of such prophets could be very close in style and situation to that of the psalmists. Humbert's study of the vocabulary and forms used throughout the Book of Habakkuk corroborates that the author moves naturally in the orbit both of the psalms and the prophets.

For the date of Habakkuk's activity, we can only glean a few clues from the book, especially a prophecy of the coming of the Chaldeans (1.6). It seems best, in my view, to take this as a genuine prediction given before the rise of Nabopolassar in 625. Thus Assyrian domination[11] was still to be reckoned with, as can well be seen in Habakkuk 2, and so Assyria is still for Habakkuk the current embodiment of oppression.

The setting where Habakkuk first launched his inspired poem may well have been a celebration of the autumn festival. For this season is indicated by the description of dearth in 3.17–19, and by the influence on the vision of the seasonal change when dry sirocco winds from eastern or southern deserts suddenly change to storms from the north and west. King and people have assembled to seek God's salvation (vv. 13,16), and Habakkuk is to tell of Yahweh's combat against chaos in the manner of the festal gospel.

We can thus posit a context where the annual rites signify the advent of Yahweh with power to rout evil forces in nature and society and to restore his people and his world. In Habakkuk we can then see a prophet who first pleads for and then is able to attest Yahweh's present will to come and to effect this salvation.

He begins with intercession, that great duty of prophets,[12] but already he is trembling with awareness of Yahweh's mighty approach:

> Yahweh, I hear the sound of you,
> I tremble, Yahweh, at your work!
> In the midst of the years make it live again,
> in the midst of the years make it known again,
> in turmoil renew work of compassion!

And now the prophet depicts the advance of God against his foes. The description begins with traits suggesting the siroccos from the southern deserts:

> God from Teman approaches,
> yes, the Holy One from the mountains of Paran.
> His splendour veils the heavens
> and the earth is filled with his radiance.
> And a glitter as of lightning appears,
> a twin-pronged weapon in his hand
> where his power hides, ready to strike.[13]
> Before him marches the Plague
> and Fever follows at his feet.
> He stands and he shakes the earth,
> he looks and he scatters the nations.
> Eternal mountains crumble,
> low fall the primeval hills
> as he makes his primeval procession.
> I see Kushan's tents sore burdened,
> buffeted the tent-walls of Midian's land.

Habakkuk thus sees the advance of God like a sirocco with weirdly bright haze, fever brought on by the evil heat, the desert wind whirling and buffeting the bedawin tents. But next he sees God's battle in terms of the rain-storms from the north-west which often follow the autumn sirocco. Or rather, he sees God's battle in terms of the old poetry which interpreted these facts of nature, poetry common in the psalms (p.7) – the raging waters personify chaos as they seem to leap against heaven and defy the missiles hurled at them from the skies. But God masters them and uses them for salvation as the life-giving waters. To Yahweh, now fearfully present, the prophet addresses his question:

> Is it against the Rivers that burns, Yahweh,
> against Rivers that burns your anger,

against Sea that burns your wrath,
that you ride with your horses,
your chariots of salvation?

Mightily awakened is your bow,
adjured are the shafts with a word,
the River-foes you cleave to the ground.

Sun, moon halt in the heights,
at the light of your arrows they flee,
at the flash of the lightning of your spear.

In wrath you tread the earth,
in anger you trample the nations.
You join combat for the salvation of your people,
for the salvation of your anointed king.

You smite the head of the evil brood,
laying him out from tail to neck.
With their own weapons you have split his followers' heads
as they whirled on to crush me
with throats craving[14] to devour the poor in their refuge.
You trample the Water-foe with your horses,
you churn the Great Waters.

So the prophet has vividly seen the Creator's defeat of chaos, the
Saviour's conquest of oppressors. Emphasizing the supernatural
power of his vision, he now tells of his own suffering in the grip
of the prophetic ecstasy:

I hear and my belly shakes,
at the din my lips quiver,
quaking seizes my bones
and my legs shudder as I walk.
I groan in the day of distress
as it rises on the host that assails us.

He concludes by affirming confidence in Yahweh as his Saviour,
– as representative of the community he could leap for joy and
bound over mountains, even though the land still lies in the state
of death:[15]

Though the fig-trees do not bud
and no fruit is on the vines,
the olive's produce fails,
the fields give no food,

13

the flocks are cut off from the fold
and the stalls without cattle,
for my part I will exult in Yahweh,
I rejoice in the God of my salvation.
The Lord Yahweh is my strength
and he makes my feet like does' feet
and upon the heights he makes me stride.

Here then we have a piece resembling the psalms but with a more explicitly visionary character, including an extended description of the seer's ecstatic state. Although the references to the current affliction of the community are not specific, the congregation would see the application to their actual needs readily enough. Thus the prophet has contributed to the festal gospel in this case by first pleading for and then presenting Yahweh's will for salvation. He has strengthened hope and faith by eloquently sharing the vision of his inner eye, the sight of Yahweh conquering evil. Thus he has authorized the present appropriation of the festal message and greatly enlivened it. But as we follow the development of the poem from incipient vision, through intercession, and so to vivid poetic portrayal of Yahweh's victory, and the final statement of confidence, we may remark above all the sacramental character of the work. As prayer can turn into a powerful word of blessing (cf. p.91), so the prophet's poetry, beginning as *t^epillā*, intercession, becomes like the prophet's symbolic actions, launching Yahweh's work into the world. It would thus be carrying further, with current application, the sacramental nature of the festal rites. We shall be able to follow up this interpretation in the texts yet to be studied.

Some of the phrases used by the prophet appear elsewhere, especially in Psalm 77. We should probably think of a prophet saturated in traditional images and words, and hence quite capable of uttering his poem spontaneously. At an appropriate point in the liturgy, ecstasy and utterance were given together. Such an utterance would then be indelibly fixed in the memory of the seer and his fellow prophets. It was found worthy of repeated use by the psalmic and prophetic choirs, rather as were the oracular psalms, and so was preserved as we have it with psalmic rubrics.

My next example of prophecy that can be related to God's festal advent is the Book of Nahum. More definitely than Habakkuk, Nahum[16] expresses the aim of Yahweh's war upon evil as directed against Assyria, though this is at first veiled by a primeval mist, as we shall see. Whether Nahum prophesied *shortly* before the doom of Nineveh in 612 B.C., or some decades earlier, is difficult to say. But that he spoke during an autumn festival is suggested by his dominant images and themes – Yahweh's advent to fight chaos ('Belial'), the messengers bringing tidings of victory with summons to fulfil vows and celebrate the pilgrimage feast.

The heading is in the manner of the prophetic books, describing the material as *massā*, oracular utterance on the destiny of 'Nineveh', capital of the Assyrian empire; it is the 'written record' of the 'visionary prophecy' of 'Nahum', native of 'Elqosh'. But at once the world of the psalms can be felt, for Nahum's opening poem (1.2–7) has an acrostic pattern, following the first half of the alphabet in the initial letters of lines. The pattern is not maintained with complete rigour; as in the case of Habakkuk, we must imagine that when the prophet is inspired to pour forth his poetry, he instinctively reproduces patterns and phrases from the psalmic and prophetic traditions in which he is saturated.

Nahum, then, will have come forward in a context of rites that symbolized God's advent as conqueror of chaos and Saviour of the oppressed. He begins to prophesy, and before indicating the aim of his prophecy he portrays the God who comes forth to combat:

A god of zeal and requital is Yahweh,
Yahweh requites and is mighty in wrath.
Yahweh requites his foes and rages against his enemies.
Yahweh is patient but great in strength
and to wink at evil is not for Yahweh.

Already, in the Hebrew, a feature of this prophesying is apparent: the words themselves are sharp weapons, forceful in their alliterations, assonances, repetitions, and rhythms. Poetry and prophecy go hand in hand. Just listen to the interplay of *n* and *q* in the opening lines:

'ēl qannō w^enōqēm yahwe, nōqēm yahwe ūba'al ḥēmā ...
w^enaqqē lō y^enaqqe yahwe.

And now (1.3b) it becomes clearer that the God who fills the prophet's vision is moving out to battle. Before his fierce majesty all the great elements of nature are utterly confounded, not least

15

the sea which (as in other festal poetry, see p.12) personifies the chaos-foe:

> In storm-wind and tempest he takes his way
> and clouds are the dust raised by his feet.
> When he thunders at the Sea he dries it up
> and all the River-foes he strikes dry.
> Mount Bashan withers, Carmel also,
> and the verdure of Lebanon withers.
> Mountains quake at him and hills dissolve,
> Earth cries out before his advance,
> the world and all its creatures.
> Before his wrath who can stand
> and who can stay in the heat of his anger?
> His fury pours forth like fire
> and the rocks are thrown down in his way.

But this fearsome portrayal ends with a note of discrimination; Yahweh is the Saviour whose advance is against the tyrant. Who this tyrant is, Nahum still does not enunciate:

> Yahweh is good,
> giving refuge in the day of distress.
> He cares for those who shelter in him
> in the overwhelming flood.
> But her sanctuary he will utterly destroy
> and his enemies he will chase into darkness.

It is to these mysterious enemies that the prophet now turns his attention, sending forth God's own words to strike them. A scornful question fixes their guilt, and then the verbal missiles fly, sharp with imagery and sound-play:

> What do you plot against Yahweh?
> He will utterly destroy.
> Opposition will not rise twice.
> Though they be tangled as thorn-bushes
> and soaked in their liquor,
> they will be consumed like dried-up stubble.

The female enemy is addressed, and reference is made to her chief abettor, the captain of the forces of darkness:

> From you has come out to battle
> the plotter of evil against Yahweh,
> Counsellor Belial.

16

It is a drama of the imagination. The foes have now come into the centre of the mental stage; against them Nahum now speaks an oracle introduced in classic fashion:

> But thus says Yahweh –
> Though they be strong,
> though they be many,
> even so they shall be cut down
> and he will pass away,
> and when I strike you [Woman]
> I shall not need two blows.

A word is then directed to Yahweh's city:

> But now I will break his yoke from off you
> and your bonds I will snap.

So back again to Belial:

> And for you Yahweh has given command –
> Let the seed of your line be sown no more,
> from the house of your gods I will cut off
> images of wood and metal,
> I appoint your grave
> for you are worthless.

The rapid changes in the person addressed certainly suggest some use of gesture and symbols to clarify the meaning. With another change, the prophet turns to Yahweh's community, again creating a new scene in his drama. Here he takes up a feature of the festival, the running of messengers before Yahweh's procession, announcing his symbolic victory:

> See, on the mountains
> the feet of the runner with tidings
> announcing that all is well!

> Celebrate your festivals, Judah,
> bring your vowed offerings,
> for never again shall Belial sweep over you,
> he is altogether destroyed!

A similar picture of the feet of the runners is used by the prophet of Isaiah 52.7, who has to predict the fall of a subsequent empire, Babylon, and there the culminating cry is:

> Your God now reigns!

17

Against the background of the psalms (cf. p.9) we can see that both prophets are interpreting the downfall of tyrants in terms of the festal gospel of the manifestation of God's kingship.

Yet Nahum has still not verbally identified the mysterious foes of Yahweh in political terms, and before he does so he will develop his visionary drama further. His excited phrases now create a vivid scene of assault upon the enemy's capital city. Thus Yahweh, having dealt with the captain Belial sent out against him in the field, now carries home the attack on the enemy's base, which eventually is identified as Nineveh, Assyrian capital and residence of the goddess Ishtar:

> The conqueror advances against you!
> Guard the ramparts,
> watch the ways,
> gird your loins,
> summon all your strength!

The prophet now goes some way to part the primeval mist which has so far covered his scenes. He states the aim of God's war as the salvation of oppressed Israel:

> Yahweh will restore the splendour of Jacob,
> the full splendour of Israel,
> for the emptiers have emptied them out
> and have ruined their branches.

And so back to the assaulting army, a fiery aspect:

> Reddened the shield of his warriors,
> scarlet-clad the men of war,
> like fire the flags of the chariots
> as they form up for the charge
> and the spears are brandished!

> Through outer streets the chariots rage,
> jolting and hurtling through the squares,
> flashing like torches,
> swift as lightnings they run.

And now the prophet sees how the divine commander re-forms his troops for the assault on the last bastion, the temple of the goddess:

18

He musters his heroes,
they stagger forward,
they hasten to her wall,
the screens are set up,
the gates of the rivers are opened,
yes, the temple dissolves and is washed away.[17]
She is made captive and led away
with her maids moaning like the sound of doves,
drumming upon their hearts.

As for Nineveh,
though her waters were like a reservoir,
now they flee –
Stop! Stop! –
but none turns back.

Plunder the silver,
plunder the gold!
No end of treasure,
piles of precious goods!
Ruin and ravaging and devastation,
and melting of hearts
and tottering of knees,
all loins writhing,
all faces discoloured.

The hectic drama now reaches stillness and finality, as the prophet contemplates the ruin which has filled his imagination and sings the dirge or death-song over it. In the funeral manner he characterizes the deceased; by doing so in terms of Nineveh's cruel ravagings of the peoples, he implies the reason for God's act:

Where, oh where is the lair of the lions
and the food for the young lions
which the lion went to fetch?
There the whelps of the lion lay
and none disturbed.
The lion tore for the appetite of his whelps
and strangled for his mates
and filled his caves with prey
and his lair with victims.

Thus far in his prophesying, Nahum has depicted Yahweh's approach against the oppressor, his routing of enemy forces in the field, his storming of the enemy capital, the captivity of the

19

goddess and the ruin of her dwelling – visions of the future, sealed with a funeral lament over a tyranny that to the visionary eye is now dead and buried.

The rest of his prophecy forms a cycle with a similar dramatic line, again creating present scenes of Yahweh advancing to combat, the fearsome word of Yahweh, the siege and storming of Nineveh, the final stillness marked by a funeral song over the Assyrian monarchy. This second cycle grows naturally from the first, taking up at once the metaphor of the tearing lion. Its special contribution is a more explicit indictment of Assyrian tyranny. But it seems that its main purpose is to double the strength of the prophet's blow against Nineveh, and again he uses every poetic resource to sharpen his verbal missiles. We get the same terse, crackling phrases and alarming actualization (3.1f.):

> Ah! murderous city,
> all deceit,
> full of plunder,
> no victim escapes!
> Listen to the whips and the thunder of wheels!
> Horses galloping, chariots bounding,
> riders urging,
> flash of blades
> and lightning of spears
> and heaps of slain, yes, piles of bodies,
> no end of corpses, they stumble over bodies.

We get the same deployment of imagery – Nineveh as the chief of harlot-witches, Nineveh compared to the great Egyptian capital destroyed by Assyria, Assyrian imperial agents compared to a plague of locusts.

Now while Nahum's message would obviously be (in accordance with his name) 'consoling' to an Israelite assembly, so much of his effort is directed to actualizing the doom of Yahweh's foe and indeed addressing that very foe, that we can conclude that our earlier suggestion was correct: such prophecy uses vision and poetry like a symbolic act, launching Yahweh's power – according to his will – against the wicked.

In a context of festal rites, then, Nahum will have given direction and heightened actuality to the theme of Yahweh's sovereignty. The supremacy of Yahweh over the chaos forces is to be manifested in his coming overthrow of Assyria, to the relief of Israel. Nahum thus authenticates a message of salvation and becomes the instrument of Yahweh's intervening power. Through his ecstatic imagination and poetic utterance the essence of Yahweh's intervention is already given birth.

From Nahum we can pass to a collection of prophecies in Jeremiah 46—51 with many of the features we have already observed. It is particularly helpful in showing how the exciting pieces in Nahum and some we have yet to study in Isaiah 40f. draw on the common stock of a certain kind of prophetic ministry.

Jeremiah 46—51 contains prophecies anticipating the doom of various nations. There are pieces against Egypt; Philistia, Tyre, Sidon; Moab, Ammon, Edom; Damascus, Kedar, and Hazor, Elam (prose), and Babylon, thus sending Yahweh's judgement round the compass from south to west, to east, to north (Babylon being north in terms of routes from Jerusalem). Salvation is announced for Israel. The collection as a whole, and several of the units, are headed as words through Jeremiah 'the prophet', and the historical background seems to be that of Jeremiah's lifetime, though we cannot be sure whether he was the author of some or all of this material. There are scarcely any indications of the setting in which such prophecy was delivered. However, the kingship of Yahweh is mentioned several times, giving the impression that his war upon these foes stigmatized as arrogant or cruel is the assertion of that kingship (46.18; 48.15; 49.38); there are indications of a decisive year (48.44) or day (46.10) and imagery of a sacrificial feast (46.10). The similarity of these pieces to those in the more coherent cycles of Nahum and Isaiah 40f. does align them with the tradition of the prophets who gave vividness and application to the festal themes.

Once again we find the prophet giving himself to be the launcher of Yahweh's war. In his ecstatic imagination the assault is already begun. He is caught up in the scenes, calling shrilly, ironically, etc. to the participants. Again we find that he uses words for the utmost effects of actuality, excitement, and power. Listen as he applies the 'day of Yahweh's requital' to the Egyptian armies confronting Nebuchadnezzar beside the Euphrates. He foretells their defeat which was in fact to occur in 604 at Carchemish, but it is only near the end of his poem that he makes clear who are to be the vanquished (46.3f.):

Line up with shields and bucklers
and close up for battle!
Harness the horses,
mount, horsemen!
Form up in helmets,
polish the spears,
put on your armour!

Oh why must I see it?
They are broken and repulsed,
their heroes beaten down,
they flee headlong, no looking back,
'Terror on every side' is the oracle of Yahweh.

No escape for the swiftest,
no deliverance for the strongest!
In the north by the River Euphrates
they stumble and fall.

The message is still mysterious. Who are the vanquished? Now
the battle is portrayed a second time, doubling the blow. The
suspense as to the identity is first heightened with a question and
then resolved (46.7f.):

Who is this, rising like the Nile,
like rivers of raging waters?
It is Egypt that rises like the Nile,
like rivers of raging waters!

(This answer was already latent in the question, for the simile of
the rivers ($y^{e'}\bar{o}r$, $n\bar{a}h\bar{a}r$) was appropriate to Egypt, as well as
suggestive of Yahweh's water-foe.)

He has boasted, I will rise,
I will cover the earth,
I will destroy cities and their inhabitants.

Charge, horses,
rage, chariots,
advance, warriors,
men of Ethiopia and Put who bear shields,
men of Lud who shoot from bows!

But this day belongs to the Lord Yahweh of Hosts,
the day of requital to requite his foes.
The sword shall devour and be sated
and drink its fill of their blood,

22

for the Lord Yahweh of Hosts keeps a feast of sacrifice
in the north country by the River Euphrates.

Only now is the outcome clarified (46.11f.):

Go up to Gilead and get balm, Miss Egypt!
In vain you use many remedies,·
your wounds will not heal.
The nations hear of your defeat,
the world resounds with your wailing,
for the warrior stumbled on his fellow
and both fell together.

Here, as in Nahum, we see the culmination taking the style of a
dirge — the enemy as good as dead. Similarly, in 48.17, the
prophet seals the doom of Moab:

Mourn him all you his neighbours
and all you his acquaintances, say
Ah, how is the powerful sceptre broken,
broken the glorious staff!

Similarly, 48.31–2:

Therefore I wail for Moab,
I cry out for all Moab,
for the men of Kir Heres I mourn,
with more than the weeping for Jazer
I weep for you, vine of Sibma....

And likewise for Damascus (49.25):

Ah, how forsaken the city of praise,
the town of my joy!

And for Babylon (50.23; cf. 51.41):

Ah, how hacked and smashed in its turn
is the hammer of all the earth!
Ah, how reduced to ruin among the nations
is Babylon!

The weapons of poetry are wielded with skill, as in the pathetic
but ironic address, such as the already quoted 'Go up to Gilead
and get balm' (46.11), or in 48.9, 'Give wings to Moab, for she
would fly away',[18] or 48.18, 'Come down from your glory and sit
on the dusty ground, Queen Dibon'. The similes and metaphors
bring out a quality in the object of Yahweh's wrath, making him

23

the more vulnerable. Puns and alliteration give extra strength, as in 48.2:

The praise of Moab is at an end,
in Hešbon *hāš^ebū* [they plan] evil against her.

Or 48.43:

Against you, Prince Moab,[19]
panic and pit and trap!
(*paḥad wāpaḥat wāpāḥ.*)

The participation of the prophet in Yahweh's war is especially vivid when he enacts Yahweh's commissioning of his weapons. The antiquity of this feature is shown by its occurrence in the Ugaritic texts,[20] where a god gives Baal's weapons the power-laden charge:

You, your name is Chaser.
Chaser, chase the Sea,
chase Sea from his throne,
River from his seat of dominion....

You, your name is Driver!
Driver, drive the Sea from his throne....

It strikes the head of the Lord Sea,
between the eyes the Lord River.

We have already met a more compact treatment of this theme in the visionary battle of Habakkuk 3 (p. 13):

Mightily awakened is your bow,
adjured are the shafts with a word,
the River-foes you cleave to the ground.

In Jeremiah 51.20f. we find a full and lurid example:

You are my mace, my weapon of war,
with you I will break nations in pieces
and with you I will destroy sovereignties
and with you I will break horse and rider
and with you I will break chariot and rider
and with you I will break men and women
and with you I will break young and old
and with you I will break youths and maidens
and with you I will break shepherd and flock
and with you I will break ploughmen and team
and with you I will break governors and commanders.

And again in 50.35f.:

This sword is against the Chaldeans — utterance of Yahweh —
and against the inhabitants of Babylon
and against her officers and wise men.
It is a sword against the diviners — they will be made fools,
a sword against her warriors — they will panic,
a sword against horses and chariots
and all the mercenaries in her midst — they will become women,
a sword against her treasures — they will be plundered,
a sword against her waters — they will be dried up!
For it is a land of idols,
they are mad with superstitions.

Address to Yahweh's weapon is found also in 47.6f.:

Ah, sword charged by Yahweh,
how long before you rest?
Get back in your scabbard,
rest and be still!

How can she rest when Yahweh has commissioned her?
Against Ashkelon and the coastland,
there has he appointed her.

However vivid the portrayals of war, we must remember that
such prophets are foretelling, as they link the liturgical
enactments of Yahweh's triumphs with future political upheavals.
Events sometimes turned out rather differently. Thus the oracles
against Babylon in Jeremiah 50—51 act out an assault and ruin
which were never in fact to take place, since in the sixth century
the Babylonian empire fell to Cyrus without assault and
destruction for the city of Babylon (cf. Jer. 51.59f.; p.27). Yet
how realistically the prophet creates the predicted scene in 50.2:

Tell all the nations,
carry the tidings, raise the signals,
carry tidings and make no secret, say
Babylon is taken,
Bel is put to shame,
Marduk is broken down,
her idols are put to shame,
her images are broken down.

25

And in verse 14:

> Line up against Babylon on all sides,
> all you that bend the bow,
> shoot at her, spare no arrows,
> for against Yahweh has she sinned!
> Raise the battle-cries against her from all sides!
>
> She throws up her hands,
> her bastions fall,
> her walls are demolished.
> Yes, this is the requital from Yahweh.
> Requite her! As she has done, do to her!

And verse 28:

> Ah, the noise of those who flee
> and escape from the land of Babylon
> to declare in Zion
> requital by Yahweh our God,
> requital for his temple!

The deriding of the god Marduk fits the pattern of thought where the kingship of Yahweh is manifested. Other gods and their images are brought low, while Yahweh is exalted as lord of nature and mankind, thus 51.11f.:

> Polish the arrows, fill the quivers!
> Yahweh has stirred the spirit of the kings of the Medes,
> for against Babylon is Yahweh's purpose, to destroy her....
>
> Against the walls of Babylon raise the standards,
> make the siege secure,
> post the watches,
> prepare the ambushes,
> for Yahweh both plans and carries out
> what he has spoken against the inhabitants of Babylon!
>
> O you who dwell by mighty waters,
> rich in treasures,
> your end has come....
>
> He who made the earth by his power,
> who established the world by his wisdom
> and by his understanding stretched out the heavens –
> when he utters his voice
> there is tumult of waters in the heavens

and he makes mists rise from the ends of the earth.
He makes lightnings for the rain
and he brings out the wind from his stores.

All men are stupid and without knowledge,
every goldsmith is shamed by his idols,
for what he casts is futile
and there is no breath in it....
Not like these in the portion of Jacob,
it is he who moulded all things
and the people for his own possession –
his name is Yahweh of Hosts.

This latter piece, 51.15f., is preserved also in 10.12–16 where it
is preceded by expressions of Yahweh's kingship, 10.6f.:

None can compare with you, Yahweh,
you are mighty and your name is mighty.
Who would not fear you, King of the nations....

But Yahweh is truly God,
he is the living God, the eternal King.

At his wrath the earth quakes
and the nations cannot withstand his rage.

The collection of Jeremiah 46—51 is concluded with an
interesting narrative. It is recounted (51.59f.) that the prophet
Jeremiah sent to Babylon a scroll of his prophecies against
Babylon with instructions that there they be read and address be
made to Yahweh as though reminding him of what he had said;
then the scroll to be weighted with a stone and sunk into the
Euphrates with the words: 'Thus shall Babylon sink to rise no
more, because of the calamity I bring upon her.'

This narrative shows how the visions and portrayals of
anticipated assaults could be aligned with the symbolic acts. The
ecstatic poetry, no less than the symbolic actions, was a veritable
blow of God against his foe.

Now as we have noted these pieces from the Jeremiah
collection, we have no doubt been struck by similarities not only
with Nahum but also with Isaiah 40—55. This latter cycle will
now give us further illustration of prophetic actualizing and
particularizing of the festal theme of Yahweh's kingly triumph.
Here the prophetic voice, sounding out between about 550 and

27

540 B.C., has to predict the fall of Babylon and the salvation of Zion and does so with a plenitude of festal tradition. The link with the old festal advents is especially clear, for the political change is imagined in terms of Yahweh's assault on his foe (42.13), derision of other gods (46, etc.), the grand procession of Yahweh as Saviour-King into Zion (40; 52), and the hymns of jubilation (42.10f.; 44.23; 52.9f.). Several scholars[21] have recently accepted that these prophecies originated in worship and posit gatherings for lament in the Babylonian Exile. It might well be that such gatherings would be convened especially at the old seasons of worship, prompting the resurgence of the prophetic work and style for those occasions.

Certainly this cycle is especially close to the world of the psalms. Thus it is out of a psalm-like utterance that a prophet develops his rather uninhibited vision of Yahweh working up frenzy for the combat (42.10f.):

Sing to Yahweh a new song,
his praise from the end of the earth,
you who sail the sea and all sea creatures,
you far coasts and your inhabitants!
Let the wilderness and its settlements raise a hymn ...
let them ascribe glory to Yahweh,
let them tell his praise on the far coasts!

Yahweh issues to combat like a champion,
like a warrior he works up his fury,
he chants his war-cry, he roars,
he menaces his foes.

Then Yahweh's oracle is pronounced (v. 14):

Too long have I been quiet,
I did nothing, I held myself back.
Now like a woman giving birth I will shriek,
gasping and panting for breath,
I will lay waste the mountains and hills
and dry up all their verdure,
I will make the rivers into coastlands
and dry up the pools....

Like Nahum and the Jeremiah collection, the cycle already sees the enemy city fallen and the images captured (46.1):

Bel bows low,
Nebo grovels,
their images are on beasts and cattle.
Your processional furniture is loaded up,
a burden for the poor beast.
Brought low and grovelling,
they [the gods] cannot rescue the burden
for they themselves have gone into captivity.

As in Nahum and Jeremiah, we hear an ironical address to the personified enemy city (47.1f.):

Come down, be seated on the dust,
Princess Babylon!
Be seated on the ground,
no throne for you, Miss Chaldea!
No more shall they call you soft-skinned and delicate....

As Nahum had assailed Nineveh as harlot-witch, now to be stripped and pilloried, so Babylon is taunted (47.12):

Stay with your spells and many sorceries
which you have worked since your youth!
Perhaps you will get them to act again,
perhaps you will frighten someone....

The humiliation of the rival gods is especially prominent in Isaiah 40—55, being, as we have seen, part of the assertion of Yahweh's supremacy; likewise the prominent treatment of his creation and control of nature and his power to determine human affairs. Especially close to the psalms is the summing-up of the message of triumph and salvation in portrayals of Yahweh's procession into Zion. We have already seen that the cycle begins with words authorizing through prophetic ministries the procession of salvation (p.9). Tidings of victory are carried to Zion (40.10f.):

See, the Lord Yahweh!
He comes as conqueror,
his own arm is ruler now!
See, he has his spoils with him
and his gains before him,
like a shepherd who herds his flock
and with his arm picks up the lambs
and carries them in his bosom
and leads the mothers to water.

29

This is the situation where the festal worshippers in Zion would see the messengers running in. I have already quoted Nahum's version (p.17). The tradition is very similar in Isaiah 52.7:

How beautiful on the mountains
are the feet of the runner with tidings,
who tells of victory,
who brings good tidings,
who tells of salvation,
who says to Zion,
Your God now reigns!

This evokes a psalm of praise (52.9–10):

Break into chants of triumph,
waste places of Jerusalem,
for Yahweh has comforted his people,
he has redeemed Jerusalem!

Yahweh has bared his holy arm
in the eyes of all the nations,
and all the ends of the earth
have seen the salvation wrought by our God.

The call to leave Babylon is joined with the thought of ritual cleansing and the processional bearing of the sacred vessels (52.11):

Away, away, come away from there,
touch nothing that defiles,
come out from the midst of her,
purify yourselves, bearers of Yahweh's vessels!
You are not to leave in panic
or rush away in flight.
At your head marches Yahweh,
yes, the God of Israel guards the rear as well.

In this procession to Zion, then, Yahweh himself is present, as he is in that of Psalms 24, 68, etc. Indeed we could almost have continued with an arrival at Zion like that of Psalm 24:

Lift up your heads, you gates,
be lifted up, eternal doors,
that the King of Glory may enter!

We do come close to such words of entry in other parts of the

Isaiah collection. This scene from the great festival is reflected, for example, in what may be a post-exilic deposit, Isaiah 26.1–2:

Now we have a mighty city,
for he has set up salvation for walls and rampart.
Open the gates that a true-hearted people may enter,
a people that keeps faith.

Likewise 62.10, perhaps from near the end of the Exile:

Pass through, pass through the gates,
prepare the way for the host,
build up, build up the highway,
clear it of stones,
lift up a standard over the peoples....

The preparing of the processional way is also a festal theme in the new-year celebrations of Marduk; at the appointed time the Babylonian king is careful to see that Marduk's 'route is made beautiful, his way renewed, the path put in order for him, the road opened'.[22]

Isaiah 62.11 continues with reference to the prophetic message which authorizes the rites of salvation:

See, Yahweh has announced to the end of the earth,
Say to Damsel Zion,
See, your salvation enters,
see, he has his spoils with him
and his gains before him....

Perhaps the most dramatic of all the visions of solemn entry is that found in Isaiah 63. The God who comes is challenged to declare his identity (rather as in Psalm 24) and to account for the crimson stains on his garments:

Who is this entering so covered in red,[23]
his garments more crimson than at grape-harvest?[24]
Who is this so gloriously apparelled,
stooping under the abundance of his trophies?

It is I who have spoken for deliverance,
I who am mighty to save.

As in Psalm 24, the questioner at the gate persists:

But why is your clothing red
and your garments like a grape-treader's?

> Alone I have trodden the wine press,
> from all the peoples no one helped me.
> Yes, I trod in my anger
> and trampled in my wrath
> that the juice spattered my garments
> and I stained all my clothing.
> For the day of my requital was in my heart
> and the year for redeeming my people had come.
> I looked, and no one would help them,
> I was astonished that none would uphold them,
> so my own arm brought salvation
> and my own fury upheld me
> and I trampled the peoples in my wrath
> and I broke them in my fury
> and I poured their juice on the ground.

In the texts I have now adduced from the prophets, we have seen how prophetic ministries gave force and application to the festal experience of Yahweh's kingship. Ecstatic prophets would interpret Yahweh's will for the current situation and yield themselves instruments in launching his war upon evil powers and portraying his triumphant entry into his temple. In particular, doom was directed at the great states of Assyria, Egypt, and Babylon, sometimes also at other states found guilty – Philistia, Moab, Edom, etc.

But if the prophets in these cases served to authorize salvation for Israel, one should conclude that the issue was at first open. It was not assumed that Yahweh came only to relieve – this would in any case belie experience. The work of a prophet was to interpret the will of God, whether favourable or otherwise, and it is to be expected that occasionally prophets might mediate a severe message in connection with Yahweh's advent. We may take this question further now by examining examples of prophets who happened to give warnings to Israel in view of the day of his coming.

The day of Yahweh as a threat to his people

Our first example is Zephaniah,[25] whom we may date between 640 and 622 B.C. His transmitted prophecies are about the same length as Nahum's, and like his consist of various units which gain effect in their sequence and patterns. There are several indications that he prophesied at the autumn festival and gave particular applications to the general message of the rites. His chief theme is the speedy approach of 'the day of Yahweh', and it appears that this day is to be the fulfilment of what was anticipated sacramentally on the day of his festal advent. Yahweh will come in universal fury against sinners (ch. 1), he will assert his kingship over all other powers (2.1—3.8), he will recreate society centred in purified Zion (3.9–20).

In the first 'act' of this universal drama (ch. 1) the oracles of threat to greedy and complacent sinners in Jerusalem are systematically set in a framework of fury upon all the world. This gives a vivid impression of Yahweh as Creator and ruler of all, yet centrally concerned with Jerusalem. The message is, on the surface, of total doom, yet the particularizing details, such as Yahweh searching with lamps through dark corners of Jerusalem for those who discount his active concern with the world, do imply discrimination in the judgement. We can sense the festal setting in the word-root which resounds several times in the opening oracle and echoes the old name of the festival, Asiph:

> 'āsōp 'āsēp kōl mē'al pᵉnē hā'ᵃdāmā, nᵉ'ūm yahwe,
> 'āsēp 'ādām ūbᵉhēmā 'āsēp 'ōp haššāmayim ūdᵉgē hayyām....

The name Asiph, Ingathering, referred to the removing or collecting in of the harvested produce in anticipation of the winter rains. Zephaniah thus ominously stresses that Yahweh's coming is to 'remove' from the face of the earth the corrupted inhabitants. Further, he uses liturgical calls and the theme of Yahweh's sacrificial feast as he stresses the dreadful aspect of the advent (1.7):

> Silence for the Lord Yahweh!
> For the day of Yahweh approaches
> and Yahweh has appointed a sacrificial feast,
> he has consecrated his invited ones.

In the second 'act' (2.1—3.8) again there is symmetry, but with the pattern reversed. This time the greater part is given to oracles against foreign nations, set in a framework of references to Zephaniah's own people. The theme now is not such unrelieved gloom. There is a fleeting chance for repentance. Mention is made of remnants that will survive. The essence of this 'act' is well expressed at its centre, 2.11:

> Yahweh reveals his dread divinity[26] over them,
> he has deflated the gods of the earth,
> that all the far coastlands of the nations
> should do homage to him, each from its sanctuary.

This is the assertion of Yahweh's kingship proclaimed in the psalms of Yahweh's throne-ascension.[27] His greatness and godhead are manifested. His rivals bow down in acknowledgement.

The surrounding oracles against foreign powers in fact tell the same story. Doom is announced[28] successively for foreign foes in the west, east, south, and north (2.4–15), and finally for sinners at the centre, Jerusalem (3.1–8). This reminds us of Egyptian festal rites of dispatching arrows and birds to the compass points in proclamation of their god's kingship over all. In these oracles Zephaniah uses poetic devices like weapons, especially the puns[29] which effect the doom implied in the names of certain towns.

Another link with the festival can be seen in the formula of general restoration used in 2.7: 'Yahweh their God will visit them and will restore them fully.'[30]Again, Zephaniah's denunciation of oppressors in Jerusalem is linked with the festal message of Yahweh's residence as Saviour in Zion. Psalm 46, for example, proclaims:

> The city of our God ...
> God is in the midst of her,
> she shall not be moved,
> God will succour her at the break of morning.

Similarly, Zephaniah 3.5:

> Yahweh in the midst of her is true,
> he will not deal corruptly,
> morning by morning he gives his justice,
> at dawn he never fails....

It is in the light of this belief in the residence of Yahweh that Zephaniah can point up the situation of sinners at Jerusalem (3.1–4):

> Woe to her that is rebellious and defiled,
> city of oppression!
> She heeds no guiding voice,
> she accepts no correction,
> she puts no trust in Yahweh,

she does not approach her God.
Her officers in her midst are roaring lions,
her rulers wolves setting off in the evening
that have not gnawed since dawn,[31]
her prophets are reckless and false,
her priests defile the holy
and abuse the sacred rulings.

In Zephaniah's third 'act' (3.9–20) a series of five units builds
up a climax of promise and hope. First the purified communion of
all peoples is foreseen, then, at the centre, the transformed Zion.
In the third of these units, 3.14–15, the prophet speaks in the style
of the festal hymns, calling for acclamation of the newly
experienced God, giving reasons that centre on Yahweh's
salvation, his destruction of Zion's foe, and his manifestation
in Zion's midst as King of Israel. The fourth unit, 3.16–18, is
in similar festal style. Zion will rejoice at the presence of Yahweh
in her midst as saving hero and ardent spouse:

Zion, do not fear,
nor let your hands be weak!
Yahweh your God is in your midst,
a hero who brings deliverance.
He will rejoice over you with merry music,
he will make poems[32] of his love.
Those driven far[33] from the festival
shall now rejoice over you with singing.
I will remove from you the day of reproach.

This 'removing' (root 'sp) may be meant to resolve at last the
discordant 'removings' of Zephaniah's opening words (p.33). The
concluding words (3.20) then take up again the formula which, as
we have noted (p.34), may summarize the meaning of the festival
as the sacrament of restoration in nature and society:

I will appoint you for a great name and praise
among all the peoples of the earth,
when I fully restore you before your very eyes, says Yahweh.

Thus in Zephaniah we see how the great festal days of Yahweh
brought visions of his ultimate day, the day of Yahweh when the
action symbolized in the liturgy would break upon the world with
full reality. The liturgy set forth Yahweh's going out to war

35

against the wicked, his assertion of his kingship over all rivals, his coming into the midst of Zion as Saviour, King and husband. It was for prophets to kindle the imaginations of the worshippers to the point of recognizing the awful reality of this message. Zephaniah fulfilled such a task. His festal message was that the ultimate drama was very near, a supreme day that was rushing upon the world; in other words, the issues linked with that day — true recognition of God and adherence to the good — were of the utmost and most immediate significance, turning the scales for life or death. He spelt out what would incur Yahweh's wrath in Jerusalem itself (not exempting priests and prophets), as well as among the peoples of the world. But he also cherished the humble and lowly, and saw the outcome of all the upheaval as the joyful reign of Yahweh from a purified Zion.

A century earlier, about 760 B.C., the prophet Amos performed a not dissimilar ministry. Again we shall see that there are indications of his prophesying in festal settings, although the record of his words is longer and more varied than Zephaniah's and includes a famous biographical narrative (ch. 7). It is related that at the royal sanctuary of Bethel he prophesied the doom of the northern dynasty and was advised by the chief priest to make good his escape to Judah and to cease prophesying at Bethel. The point of Amos' reply was to stress that he was on Yahweh's errand — it was with Yahweh that the reckoning would have to be made. The King James Version (1611) sensibly renders 'I was':

> I was no prophet, neither was I a prophet's son, but I was an herdman and a gatherer of sycomore fruit, and the Lord took me as I followed the flock, and the Lord said unto me, Go, prophesy unto my people Israel.

Taking account of the emphatic counterpoint of 'I' and 'the Lord' ('Yahweh'), we understand Amos to say that it was not *he* who chose to be a prophet; for himself, he was content with his work among flocks and fruit-trees, till Yahweh had taken hold of him and appointed him as a *nabi*-prophet[34] to Israel.

At the outset of the collection we see a striking similarity with Zephaniah 2—3 in that a series of doom words[35] is launched against foreign peoples around the compass (north-east, south-west, north-west, south-east) and then against Israel in the centre. That this scheme belongs to Yahweh's assertion of his kingship

36

from Zion is here made all the clearer by the introductory verse:

Yahweh roars from Zion
and from Jerusalem he utters his voice
and the pastures of the shepherds mourn
and the head of Carmel withers.

Like Zephaniah, then, Amos apprehended the great and imminent judgement over and above the festal triumph, and he specified objects of Yahweh's fury at home as well as abroad. His collection also, like Zephaniah's, incorporates several pieces of psalmodic character (4.13; 5.8–9; 9.5–6), proclaiming the power of Yahweh as sole ruler and Creator of the great elements. Like Habakkuk, he intercedes for Israel, but finally is told that Yahweh will hear no more – the *end* has been reached (8.1–2). Here there is a pun, which may be compared with Zephaniah's ominous play[36] with the name of the festival and its agricultural season (p. 33). Amos' vision of late-summer fruit, *qayiṣ*, suggests the season of the festival but also the 'end', *qēṣ*, which is coming for 'my people Israel'.

It is especially interesting for our present inquiry that Amos gives an explicit interpretation of the festal hope (5.18f.). The congregation yearn for the salvation of the day of Yahweh, that full dawning of the reality glimpsed in the festival. Amos interprets it with all possible stress on the fury of Yahweh against the sinners whom he has identified in Israel. Moreover, these sinners seem to be characteristic of the whole assembly, so that this prophet cannot declare Yahweh's favourable acceptance of their worship and offerings. Yahweh is not pleased with them. He does not find in them sincere repentance. He rejects them and their festal offerings of music and sacrifice. Only for a repentant people could the festal message 'Yahweh is with us' be true (5.14).

The ministry of Amos was thus especially severe towards Israel, but we can still see it as exercised in the festal setting, an example of a customary prophetic role where the prophet gives or withholds Yahweh's acceptance and qualifies and particularizes the festal message. Thus Amos confirms that the kingship of Yahweh is to be asserted, the fuller reality of his day is to come – but you, you as you are, are liable to be counted among his enemies, despite your show of worship.

But as in the record of Zephaniah, so in that of Amos, the last chapter passes from doom to restoration. It will long be debated whether Amos himself could have had occasion and will to speak such hopes. But the text at least suggests that the collectors were accustomed to a prophetic ministry which could predict both doom and subsequent restoration. Such a ministry would be the more fruitful, since a people totally without a hope can surely come to no good. The collectors have offered us an Amos who, like their Zephaniah, Hosea, Isaiah, Micah, Jeremiah, and Ezekiel, destroys that he may build (9.8f.):

See, the eyes of the Lord Yahweh
are on the reign that is sinful,
and I will destroy it from the surface of the earth.
Yet the house of Jacob I will not wholly destroy, says Yahweh,
for see, I am commanding and I will sift
among all the nations and the house of Israel,
as one shakes with a sieve
and no pebble falls to the ground.
With the sword shall die
all the sinners of my people that say,
Calamity will not reach or break through among us.

The next oracle may intend an allusion to the 'booth' rites at the festival (later known as Booths), 9.11–12:

In that day I will raise the fallen booth of David
and repair its damaged walls
and raise up what had been pulled down
and build it up as in the days of old,
that they may possess the remnant of Edom
and all the nations over which my name is invoked,
says Yahweh who achieves this.

Restoration is especially associated with fertility, in keeping with the nature of the autumn festival; it is promised that the winter rains will start with no delay (9.13f.):

See, days are coming, says Yahweh,
when hardly have harvesters finished than ploughmen start,
and hardly have grape-treaders finished than sowers start,
and the mountains shall drip with juice of grapes
and the hills will flow,
and I will wholly restore my people Israel.

And they shall build up the ruined cities and reside in them,
and they shall plant vineyards and drink their wine,
and they shall make gardens and eat their fruit,
and I shall plant them on their soil,
and they shall not be uprooted again from their soil
which I have given them, says Yahweh your God.

We have now seen much prophetic material in relation to the festal advent of God depicted in the psalms. Extracts have been drawn from Habakkuk, Nahum, Jeremiah, the later 'Isaiahs', Zephaniah, and Amos. It has, I hope, become apparent that the prophetic collections afford much evidence of a prophetic ministry which helped to actualize and apply the festal themes in weal and woe and attained in some cases true greatness of spirit. While liturgy provided a sacrament of Yahweh's coming, it could be cause as well for trembling as for rejoicing. It was for prophets to draw out the meaning most appropriate to the occasion.

2 God's Address to his Covenanted People

*Psalms expressing the epiphany and
covenantal speech of God*

The second element of worship relevant to prophecy is the
situation where the assembled people are addressed by God as
their covenant Lord, who thus recreates the basic bond with
much exhortation and testifying. Here we may begin to draw on
the material in the psalms which links most directly with the
prophets, namely the abundant speeches of God in the first
person. Our present concern is with those psalms which begin
with portrayal of God's great epiphany to his congregation, then
lead immediately into a weighty address by this manifest God to
his people.

Psalm 81 marks the epiphany clearly in verses 2–6/1–5, calling
for the full acclamation:

> Shout acclaim to God our glory,
> give the cries of triumph for the God of Jacob,
> make music and sound the drums,
> sweet harps with the lutes,
> blow the horns as for the new moon,[1]
> as for full moon, on the day of our festival!
> For this feast is a statute for Israel,
> a custom for the God of Jacob,[2]
> an observance which he enjoined on Joseph
> when he came out from the land of Egypt.[3]

After this recognition of the presence of the covenant Lord, what
more natural than that he should speak to his people as in the first
days of the relationship? The four mysterious words at the end of
verse 6/5 are best taken as a formula of transition, whereby the
minister who is now to be Yahweh's prophet or mouthpiece
announces his inspiration:

> A language I did not know
> I begin to understand.

Similarly abrupt formulae of introduction to inspired speech are
found in Psalms 95.7c; 85.9/8; Isaiah 5.9, etc. As in the case of

40

Habakkuk 3 (p. 14), we can take it that what was first given as a
new inspiration was preserved and re-used as a classic utterance.
The speech of God is now conveyed in the first person and
maintained so almost to the end of the psalm. God addresses his
people as a singular, the same corporate 'person' that he saved
from Egypt. He uses key phrases from the tradition of the Ten
Commandments (v. 10/9):

> There shall be no alien god with you
> and you shall not fall down before a foreign god.
> I am Yahweh your God
> who brought you up from the land of Egypt.
> Only open wide your mouth
> and I will fill it full!

God's desire to give abundance to his people is matched by sober
recognition of their waywardness. Note the tone of verse 9/8:

> Hear, my people, as I admonish you!
> Israel, if only you would listen to me!

And verse 12/11:

> But my people did not listen to my voice,
> Israel was not obedient to me
> and I sent them away in the stubbornness of their heart,
> they proceeded in their own devices.
> If only my people would now heed me,
> if only Israel would go forward in my ways!
> In no time I would subjugate their foes....
> – And he would feed him with the fat of the wheat –
> Yes, with honey from the rock I would feed you full.

Now from this great psalm much is already evident. Here is a
kind of prophetic ministry in the festal worship, coming into
action in the moment of Yahweh's epiphany as covenant Lord.
The excitement of the music and chanted formulae of praise is
suddenly succeeded by the warning formula: inspiration is
present, Yahweh's mind towards his people is to be declared. The
words are presented as from the mouth of Yahweh who is face to
face with the corporate and ever-living Israel. The classic themes
of the covenant are stated – the salvation, the requirements, the
rich but conditional promises. Such prophecy is no mere
divination or reading of omens, but worthy of a Moses, Samuel,

or Elijah, though the style is pure poetry in the psalm tradition.

It is remarkable that Psalm 95 has just the same structure and tone as Psalm 81, with the additional interest that the epiphany prelude is in the manner of the psalms proclaiming Yahweh's new reign. So here the link between the dramatic presence of Yahweh in the festival and his speech as covenant Lord is all the clearer. The God whom worshippers there experience as the conqueror and saviour taking up his reign, he it is who so speaks. First, then (95.1–7), the acclamation of God manifest in royal supremacy:

> Come, let us shout acclaim to Yahweh,
> let us give the triumph-cries for the Rock that saves us,
> let us come before his face with acknowledgement,
> with music and chant let us acclaim him!
> For Yahweh is the supreme God,
> yes, the Great King over all the gods,
> to whom belong the remotest parts of the earth
> and the peaks of the mountains also.
> He owns the sea, having made it himself,
> he owns the dry land, for his own hands moulded it.
>
> Enter, that we may bow low and do homage,
> let us kneel before Yahweh our maker,
> for he alone is our God
> and we are the people that he shepherds,
> the flock that he tends.

And now we hear the transition to God's speech (v. 7c) – as in Psalm 81, a short phrase without parallelism:

> This very day, – if only you would listen to his voice!

Then the speech is conveyed in the first person (vv. 8–11). The tone is wholly sombre: they should not be callous towards God, lest they perish like their fathers in the wilderness.

> Do not harden your heart as happened at the Place of Dispute,
> on that day in the wilderness at the Place of Trial,
> when your fathers tried me,
> tested me – and saw what I could do.
> For forty years I grew sick of that generation.
> And I said, These are a wayward people,
> these do not understand my ways.
> So then I vowed in my wrath,
> Never shall these come to my pleasant land!

On this ominous note the psalm ends. The threat of doom for a whole generation has been revived. So again we see a stern and exacting prophecy from the old covenant tradition set within the festal worship of Yahweh as manifest King over the gods.

Psalm 50 differs from Psalms 81 and 95 in not having such acclamation and transition to divine speech. Instead we have from the outset announcement that God is speaking and summoning and addressing his subjects; but still the announcements are interwoven with wonderful descriptions of his present epiphany at Zion:

> God of gods, Yahweh speaks
> and summons the world
> from the rising of the sun to its setting.
> Out of Zion, perfection of beauty,
> God gives his radiance,
> our God has come and is not silent,
> fire before him consumes
> and around him tempest rages.
> He summons the heavens above
> and the earth to the judgement of his people.

In verse 5 God's own voice is heard, but the main speech begins in verse 7 and continues till the end:

> Gather my covenanters before me,
> those who share in my covenant through meal of sacrifice!

> – Now the heavens affirm his righteousness
> for God himself is judge (Obeisance!) –

> Listen, my people, and I will speak,
> heed, Israel, as I admonish you!
> The God that is your God am I.

The first admonition is teaching about sacrifice. No blame now can be given about its performance. But beware of thinking that you, creatures, thereby sustain God or can bribe him – he has plenty already with the wild beasts which are his property! He does especially value the sacrifices made with public testimony to answered prayer – when you have been helped, do not neglect to offer what you promised when in need!

> Not for your sacrifices would I fault you,
> nor your burnt-offerings, which you regularly present.

43

But I cannot be bribed[4] with an ox from your shed
or goats from your pens,
for I own all the creatures of the forests,
the beasts on mountains where herds roam,
in my care are all the birds of the mountains
and I own all that moves in the open field.
If I am hungry I need not tell you,
for I own the wide earth and all that fills it.
Need I eat the flesh of your bulls
or drink the blood of your goats?

Sacrifice to God for a testimony
and fulfil for the Most High the offerings you vow,
for if you have cried to me in the time of need,
when I deliver you, you must give the glory to me.

Now (v. 16f.) comes a sharper admonition, preceded by an
introduction reminding us a little of the prophetic 'Thus says the
Lord'. The admonition seems to be addressed to any person
breaking the ethical standards of the Ten Commandments:

And to the wicked man God says,
What do I care if you tell over my statutes
and take my covenant upon your mouth
but in practice you reject discipline
and you toss my commands behind your back?
If you see a thief you abet him,
and you have a share with adulterers,
you stretch your mouth to evil
and your tongue you yoke with falsehood,
sitting with others you malign your brother,
on your own mother's son hang a calumny.

Such things you have done and should I be silent?
Do you imagine I am no better than yourself?
I will reprove you and make open reckoning with you.
Consider this, all you who forget God,
lest I snatch you away and none can deliver you.

The final word (v. 23) is positive and goes back to the previous
topic:

He who sacrifices in testimony gives the glory to me
and takes the right way.
I will fill him full with divine salvation.

In these psalms, then, we find a prophetic ministry giving

expression to the admonitions of God manifest before his gathered people. The messages are weighty and balance the divine care and provision with the requirements of devotion and obedience accompanied by sharp threats. We have now to examine some passages in the prophets which can be related to this ministry.

God's speeches of covenantal judgement in the prophets

We may take our first example from Isaiah 1, headed as 'the vision of Isaiah...'. At the outset (v. 2) heaven and earth are summoned as witnesses to Yahweh's complaint against his rebellious children, Israel:

> Hear, you heavens,
> listen, earth,
> for it is Yahweh who speaks!
>
> The children I nurtured and reared
> have rebelled against me....

The calling of heavens and earth as witnesses is an old feature of covenant ceremony.[5] One is struck by the solemnity and grand scale of the scene. Surely the prophet is calling the covenanted community to account at a great representative gathering in confrontation with Yahweh. This impression is strengthened by the similarity with Psalm 50 which, as we have seen (p. 43), suits ceremonies of covenant at the chief festival ('God of gods, Yahweh speaks and summons the world from the rising of the sun to its setting ... he summons the heavens above and the earth to the judgement of his people').

A variety of formal units follows in Isaiah 1, and it may be, as is often concluded, that they are collected from different occasions. Yet they all fit the same situation of the grand confrontation of Yahweh and the worshipping assembly of Israel and maintain a general continuity of thought. There are elements of dialogue between the covenant Lord and his people, such as we shall study in detail in our next chapter. In verse 4 the prophet delivers a 'Woe' against the nation, characterizing them as forsakers of Yahweh. In verses 5–8 he depicts their sufferings, not as a lament to move God, but in exhortation to the nation to

45

repent and be healed. Verse 9 rounds off with a switch to 'we' speech, resembling a congregational thanksgiving:

> If Yahweh of Hosts had not left us a remnant
> we should soon have been like Sodom,
> we should have resembled Gomorrah.

We may compare the communal Psalm 124:

> If Yahweh had not been for us, let Israel now say,
> if Yahweh had not been for us when men arose against us,
> then they would have swallowed us alive
> when their anger blazed against us.

The reference of the 'we' speech to Sodom and Gomorrah brings a fresh rejoinder from Yahweh (Isa. 1.10f.):

> Hear the word of Yahweh, rulers of Sodom,
> hear the teaching of our God, people of Gomorrah!
> What good to me is the abundance of your sacrifices, says Yahweh,
> I have had my fill of whole offerings of rams
> and the fat of prime beasts,
> I am not pleased with the blood of your bulls,[6] sheep, and goats....

As in Psalm 50, God's speech to his assembled covenanters considers the acceptability of their present acts of worship. Coming together to the temple in due season, bringing offerings, uttering prayers – all is unacceptable to Yahweh from people who are unrepentant sinners and corrupters of justice. Isaiah's condemnation is strong, but hardly more so than that of, say, Psalm 95 which threatened the congregation with the fate of the wilderness generation that had sickened Yahweh (p. 42). This Isaiah speech, like that of Amos 5 (p. 37), can be seen as in the tradition of the ministers who had to declare Yahweh's reaction to the offerings.[7] Displeasure is declared, but, again as in the case of Amos 5.14–15, reconciliation is offered, an appeal for true purification here in language of ritual association (Isa. 1.16):

> Wash and be cleansed!
> Put away the evil of your deeds from before my eyes....

Yahweh's oracle in verse 18 well brings out the aspect of dialogue in the festal worship, the theme being again true purification and atonement:

Come now, let us argue it through together, says Yahweh.
If your sins are as scarlet,
they shall become white as snow,
if they are red as crimson,
they shall become like wool.

The continuation (vv. 19–20) is very reminiscent of God's festal speech in Psalm 81. Thus Isaiah 1.19f.:

If you are willing and pay heed
you shall eat the good produce of the land,
but if you refuse and rebel
you will be eaten by the sword,
so speaks the mouth of Yahweh.

And Psalm 81.12/11f.:

But my people would not heed my voice
and Israel was not willing
and I sent them away ...
If only my people would heed me
and Israel walk in my ways ...
— he would feed him with the fat of the wheat —
yes, with honey from the rock I would feed you full!

In Isaiah 1.21–3 the prophet depicts the corruption of justice in Jerusalem in the style of a dirge, a form we have already met frequently (pp. 19, 23). The point of the present one is the reversal of Zion's ideals, the fall from the glory depicted in the festal hymns of Zion as residence of the newly entered King Yahweh. Point and style thus resemble Zephaniah 3.1–5 (p. 34), and, also as in Zephaniah, the sequence is an oracle of hope for a purified remnant and a restored Zion (Isa. 1.24–31).

Thus this chapter gives us samples of Yahweh's speeches to his assembled worshippers, along with associated prophetic forms. In some of the material we can just detect the historical conditions after 701 and the devastation caused by the Assyrian invasion. The prophet lives in a momentous period and conveys earnest and radical judgements, but striving always to induce repentance and sustaining ultimate hope. His subject is solely Yahweh's relation to his people, which is 'Israel', but also the assembly of worshippers in the sacred city 'Zion', and his 'children'.[8] At Zion the festal congregation encounters Yahweh. They meet for frank mutual exchanges. But as in Psalms 50, 81, and 95, so in Isaiah 1 it is Yahweh's assessment of his covenanted people which dominates. Through his minister he declares the people to be rebellious and corrupt, and as such they cannot find favour and acceptance with their worship. The desire of Yahweh to bless echoes all the same in both psalms and Isaiah. Thus Psalm 95.7:

This very day, – if only you would listen to his voice!

And Psalm 81.9/8f.:

Israel, if only you would listen to me....
If only my people would now heed me....
yes, with honey from the rock I would feed you full.

And Isaiah 1.19:

If you are willing and pay heed
you shall eat the good produce of the land.

Another prophetic passage where Yahweh's criticism of his people is put in forms of 'disputation' and mutual argument is Micah 6. Once again, the people have little to say and the main effect of the 'dispute' is to express Yahweh's exhortations. First the prophet calls to the people:

Hear now what Yahweh says,
stand up and debate before the mountains
and let the hills hear your voice!

Then to the witnesses:

Hear, you mountains, the dispute of Yahweh,
hear, you enduring ones, foundations of the earth,
for Yahweh has a dispute with his people
and he would exchange argument with Israel.

And now the mediation of Yahweh's own words:

My people, what have I done to you
and how have I wearied you? Accuse me!
Surely I brought you up from the land of Egypt
and redeemed you from the house of slaves
and sent Moses before you, and Aaron and Miriam.
My people, remember how Balak, king of Moab planned
and what answer he got from Balaam, son of Beor,
remember the way from Shittim to Gilgal
that you may acknowledge the saving acts of Yahweh.

The criticism here is not very explicit. Perhaps it follows a traditional line of rejoinder to a complaining people. In verses 6–7 a question is put from the side of the people. In topic and form it is such as would be put to a cultic authority, one who would give a ruling from Yahweh on the basis of revealed knowledge. It shows us how such 'disputes' could proceed – an abashed people inquires how it may regain the favour of Yahweh and will then be answered through the prophet. However, in the present case the questions seem designed only to set up the prophet's teaching.[9] It is as though he said: 'And if you ask, What more can we do to please Yahweh, must we carry our sacrifices to the extreme? – the answer is, No, look again at your way of life and fulfil the old requirements of justice and love and responsibility to your God in all things – this is what will please him and bring you his blessings.'

There follows a passage of more specific condemnation and threats from Yahweh (Mic. 6.9f.):

Listen, Yahweh is calling to the city....
Shall I condone dishonest balances
or the bag of deceitful weights....

For our next example, Isaiah 6, we need to recall that the autumn festival involved a dramatic manifestation of Yahweh as King. He vanquished his foes and made procession to his temple-palace. There he sat on his throne, robed in majesty, amid proclamation of his new reign of righteous salvation. There, too, he 'judged', issuing decrees and making assessment of his people. The relevant ceremonies and symbols of the earthly worship were reflections of his royal ascent above the heavens. In his temple on earth all cried 'Glory!' in unison with the heavenly beings who were then prostrating themselves before the God enthroned over the heavenly ocean (Ps. 29). Thus, in the sanctuary, 'the gate of heaven' (Gen. 28.17), the rapt worshipper ascended through the symbol to its reality.

So it could happen that at the time of the proclamation of Yahweh's kingship by the rites of solemn advent, by the eloquent visionary psalms, by the blast of the horns and the clouds of incense – so it could happen that the divine and royal presence of which all the worshippers were aware could become overwhelmingly visible to one of the visionary seers. In trance-like state Isaiah the *nabi*-prophet saw Adonay, the Lord of all, sitting as King on his exalted throne in the Holy of Holies, his robes flowing down to fill the temple. The visionary scene at first is one of acts of worship and points to the vision having arisen amid the festal praises.[10] As though in unison with the earthly choirs, the heavenly beings sing responsively. Their theme of God's holiness and world-filling glory would certainly fit the moment of supreme epiphany. The thunderous acclamations, which seem to rock the very building, and the dense clouds of smoke would correspond to the festal *t͑erū'ā* (the triumphant acclamations) and use of incense in sign of the epiphany. The action of the seraph with the burning coal may correspond to some ritual act of purification, where it would be a human servant of Yahweh who/took the priestly tongs and applied a charcoal from the altar of incense to an object to be purified.

After the cleansing, the prophet is able to take part in the next phase: the deliberations of Yahweh's council. Comparison with the vision of Micaiah (1 Kings 22) shows the traditional framework of the experience, while further afield, especially in Mesopotamia and Ugarit, we have other examples of conferences of the celestial beings. In Babylon[11] we know of the divine assembly which met before and after Marduk's royal triumph in the new-year festival and which appointed destinies. Isaiah's account could indicate that after the manifestation and acclamation of Yahweh's royal splendour there followed acts of the new reign – decisions and utterances of the King (cf. Ps. 93.5), which, however, occur in a setting of deliberation in his royal council. Thus Yahweh asks, 'Whom shall I send and who will go for us?' The prophet offers himself for the errand and is told, 'Go, and say to this people. ...' Note 'to this people' – the chapter never specifies which people. This may show that deliberation on Israel's destiny was traditionally expected here and that the assembled people is at hand, awaiting the decree. On the occasion of Psalm 65 Yahweh decreed a year of his favour, *š͑enat ṭōbāt͑ekā* (v. 12/11); he 'crowned', that is, inaugurated it. On the occasion of Psalm 85 the minister listened and reported, 'he speaks *šālōm*', he has decreed a year of bounty (v. 9/8). But in the present case the pronouncement was for ruin and calamity. Isaiah's 'How long, Lord?' briefly indicates his taking up of the traditional intercessory role of prophetic ministers, but like the interceding Amos (7.1–6), he was to find that a point had been reached where the decree of doom could not be turned aside. The particular reasons why this festal message was recorded in this way are not hard to find. The message is of the utmost gravity, but is not expected to find receptive ears. The prophet has therefore deposited the details of his experience and message so that it will one day be apparent that he has truly delivered the word of Yahweh.

A neighbouring chapter, Isaiah 5,[12] can also be seen as a festal message, though of a peculiar and intriguing style. The prophet here mediates between Yahweh as bridegroom and Israel-Zion as bride. As the groom's 'friend', that is, best man, the prophet brings on his behalf a love-song to his bride. The love-song, however, turns out to be an accusation[13] of infidelity:

I sing on behalf of my friend,
I sing my dear friend's song about his vineyard....

The vineyard is an image of the loved one. Description of her beauty might well have followed the opening statement that the vineyard was on a 'horn' or high sweep of hill green with luxuriant olive trees. But the song passes from the friend's loving care to his bitter disappointment; his vineyard gave him not sweet grapes but sour wild ones, and so he was minded to finish with his vineyard. Thus in a kind of acted parable, Isaiah mediates a message to Yahweh's festal bride,[14] Zion, that she has earned his wrath. He has waited for the fruit of mišpāṭ (justice) and look, mišpāḥ (cruelty); for ṣᵉdāqā (fair dealing) and look, ṣᵉ'āqā (a cry of anguish).

Amos 5 has already been discussed in relation to Yahweh's advent (p. 37). Following our study of Isaiah 1, we see the more clearly how Amos 5 conveys the festal judgement. Like Isaiah, Amos has to declare the present festal offering of praises, psalmody, and offerings unacceptable. Yahweh has assessed them as a people still adhering to oppression and injustice and therefore rejects their pilgrimage, will not smell with favour the smoke and incense, shuts his ears to their psalms (Amos 5.21–3). If they would become seekers of good and not evil, they would have the festal gifts of life and salvation, and the festal cry 'Yahweh is with us' (cf. Ps. 46.8/7) would come true (5.14). The worshippers yearn for Yahweh's greater day, the full realization of the

51

blessings delineated in the festival, the day of the full light of salvation. But the festal judgement which Amos conveyed warned that these worshippers, as they were, would be reckoned among the enemies of Yahweh at his coming.

Amos 9 is also relevant to our subject, especially when related to our study of Isaiah 6 (p. 49). The entranced Amos sees Adonay, the Lord of all, as manifest in his sanctuary, which here may be Bethel. High above the altar God has taken up his position for judgement. Heavenly ministers must be awaiting the decree of the divine King. Below in the temple building are crowded the dignitaries of the congregation, eagerly expecting the mediation of the pronouncement. Will he speak for them a good destiny, a year of *šālōm*? He speaks, commanding an attendant:

Smite the capitals that the thresholds quake,
shattering them on the heads of all,
and survivors I will slay with my sword!
Not a fleer of them shall flee,
not an escaper of them shall escape....

A final example of the tradition of Yahweh's festal speech may be taken from Isaiah 48. Even in the Exile, as already mentioned (p. 28), there will have been gatherings of the congregation and no doubt in relation to the old seasons. The circles of prophetic ministers were able still to maintain their tradition and on these occasions to speak for Yahweh to his covenanters in the traditional style. And this is what we find in Isaiah 48, beginning 'Hear this, house of Jacob'. In verses 17–19 we are struck by the similarity to the festal speech of Psalm 81 (p. 41):

Thus says Yahweh ...
I am Yahweh your God
who teaches you to profit
and leads you in the way you should go.
If you had but heeded my commandments,
your prosperity would have been like a river
and your provision like the waves of the sea....

Let us now summarize all our impressions of Yahweh's speeches as covenant Lord to assembled Israel. We have observed a continuity between several great psalms and chapters in Isaiah, Micah, Amos, and Deutero-Isaiah. Both psalms and prophets evidence the same impressive ministry, where a poetic speaker articulates the mind of Yahweh when his presence has been signified in the cult. The speeches express God's generous love, but also his requirements. The warning tone predominates and sometimes reaches sharp condemnation. But we need not posit a peculiar, separate type of doom-prophet. All the examples are variations on the common pattern of God's grace and demand.

3   Dialogue of God and Congregation

Lamenting appeal and answering oracle in the psalms

In addition to the covenantal addresses treated in Chapter 2, we may distinguish a characteristic situation in Israelite worship where appeal was made to God and answer given. While the occasion might be a special convocation in a day of emergency (cf. Judg. 20.23; 2 Chron. 20), regular festal gatherings too could include such dialogue of people and God; for the season when he so 'came near' and 'let himself be found' (Isa. 55.6) was clearly a suitable time to voice the people's needs. The contrast between the ideal state proclaimed in the festal liturgy and current afflictions could give a sharp edge to the intercessions.

We have to expect that prophetically gifted[1] ministers led in the appeals to God as well as bringing back his response. For it was the same gift of intimacy that was needed, whether to draw near to him with a moving request, or to bring a word from his inner council.

In the Psalter, therefore, we have to look for psalmists of prophetic gifts not only in the passages conveying the replies of God, but also in the numerous moving appeals, often formed as 'laments'. The laments were aimed at getting a response from God and so in any case were linked with oracles of prophecy; but, beyond this, we acknowledge that appeals, as well as answers, were tasks for charismatic resources.

Turning to examples of such dialogic worship in the Psalter, we may instance Psalm 60. Here we meet first a lament of the community ('we', vv. 3–7/1–5), portraying to God the severity of the hardship which he has sent upon his beloved people, and concluding:

Save with your right hand and answer us!

Answer is indeed given[2] (vv. 8–10/6–8) in an oracle which perhaps reaffirms a classic oracle – God is victor and master and rules through his chosen people. Note the introductory formula:

God speaks in his sanctuary [*or* in his holy epiphany]!

Then follows his direct speech:

I exult as I portion out Shechem....

But this grand statement is not received too meekly. The liveliness of the dialogue in Israelite worship is here illustrated. The community makes a sharp rejoinder, or rather, one is made on their behalf (v. 12/10):

But is it not yourself, God, who are spurning us,
and you, God, who are not going out to battle with our hosts?
Do give us help against the enemy
for human help is futile!
By God alone we shall fight valiantly,
he it is who will trample on our foes.

The apparently classic oracle cited in this psalm is cited also in Psalm 108. Here, too, it provides the answer to lamenting prayer, only to be followed by further protest, finally resolved in a statement of trust.

Lamenting prayer and prophetic answer are also found in Psalm 85. The opening is puzzling in that it seems already to acknowledge God's favour and forgiveness. It is possible that the perfect tenses here are 'precative', giving (vv. 2–4/1–3) 'Yahweh, accept your land, fully restore Jacob, [etc.]' Otherwise the reference could be either to some great salvation given in years gone by, or to the present ritual in which forgiveness would have been signified but anxiety remained about the practical outcome. At all events, in the next section (vv. 5–8/4–7) the community implores God for mercy and relief. A prophetic minister then states (v. 9/8):

I will listen for what the God Yahweh will say –
yes, he pronounces for prosperity!

And so the message unfolds (indirectly reported). Warning against folly is included, but the message is otherwise of a bountiful year to come. The expression is highly imaginative – a vision of angels who personify blessings, embracing, kissing, springing up from the ground, leaning out of heaven's windows, marching as heralds before Yahweh.

Another example of dialogue is Psalm 12. The people's spokesman pleads with God for salvation, lamenting the falsehood and evil which afflict society and vividly depicting the cunning trickery and arrogance of the wicked. The answering oracle (v. 6/5) is direct speech of God accompanied by the formula 'says Yahweh':

Because of the plundering of the poor
and the groaning of the needy
now I will arise, says Yahweh.
I will place in safety
him for whom pursuers pant.

To this oracle there is a rejoinder (v. 7/6f.), welcoming and appreciating Yahweh's words and expressing trust, though not without further indicating how direful the situation is:

The words of Yahweh are pure words,
silver refined in a furnace,
purified seven times on to the ground.
You, Yahweh, will fulfil them,
you will preserve him always from this generation.
The wicked prowl all around us
and vileness is exalted among mankind.

Rather similar is Psalm 14. However, here the opening description of evil times seems not so much a lament to God as a diagnosis by his prophetic spokesman, who can even add his knowledge that Yahweh has leaned over and gazed down searchingly from heaven to see if any of mankind were true worshippers, innocent of cruelty and corruption, but (v. 3) had found, alas, that

All of them have gone astray
and become corrupt,
there is none that does good,
no, not one.

There follows a short oracle (v. 4) in the form of an ominous question:

Have none of the evil-doers understanding,
that they eat my people
as they eat bread?

Not surprisingly, this terse oracle is then amplified (v. 4b) with prophetic authority (God in third person):

They have not called on Yahweh.
There they shall tremble with fright,
for God is in the company of the righteous.
In the anguish of the poor[3]
you shall meet your downfall,
for Yahweh is his refuge.

The rejoinder to this message from God is a concluding supplication in hopeful tone:

If only the salvation of Israel would come from Zion!
When Yahweh fully restores his people,
Jacob will rejoice,
Israel will make merry.

These examples where both lament and answering oracle have been preserved help us to understand how other laments which stand on their own were in fact seeking an answer from God. One great lament, Psalm 74, mentions (v. 9):

We see no signs for us,
there is no longer a *nabi*-prophet,
no one in our gathering who knows how long.

Thus there were times of deepest distress when no answer came through the oracles. Yet we must remember that these laments also were part of the tradition of dialogue, skilful intercessions by gifted orders, part of the worship where prophetic voices were to announce God's answer if he so willed.

Such communal laments, then, preserve one side of the dialogue in worship, the congregation's appeal to God. Psalm 82 may be an example of the preservation of the other side – the divine revelation through the prophet, without the preceding appeal. The bulk of this psalm is the revelation of the divine decision against the oppressors, but the last verse does give us the community's reaction; on their behalf is voiced an appeal for realization of the vision, and so we have part of the fuller pattern. The seer introduces the direct speech of God not with a 'Thus says God' or the like, but with a portrayal of God preparing to give sentence in his heavenly council:

God presides in the divine council,
in the midst of the gods he judges.

Like the prophets Micaiah, Isaiah, and Amos (pp. 50–2), the

57

psalmist-seer has been granted vision and hearing to know of
God's plans and actions forming in his heavenly council; like
Amos (9.1) he begins his account by telling of God's taking his
position as King and Judge. Then he reproduces God's own
speech to members of his council:

> How long will you govern unjustly
> and show favour to the wicked?
> I commissioned you to rule[4] for the weak and fatherless,
> to give justice to the lowly and poor,
> to deliver the weak and impoverished,
> to save them from the hand of the wicked.
>
> They have no sense, no wisdom,
> in darkness they come and go,
> all the foundations of the earth give way.
>
> I decree[5] that though you are gods
> and all of you sons of the Most High,
> yet like mankind you shall die,
> like any human governor you shall fall.

God's speech has now ended. The seer's account of the hidden
event has brought hope that the anarchy of violence and
selfishness among the nations will no longer be tolerated by the
supreme God. The response of the worshippers is now expressed
as a prayer for the realization of the vision. May the heavenly
delegates, to whom the corruption is ascribed, be swept aside and
the supreme God rule directly, his justice unimpeded:

> Arise, God, rule the world directly,
> yes, you yourself take over all the nations!

The dialogue of God and people in the prophets

A similar ministry of voicing the dialogue of God and people is
quite well represented in the prophetic books. Habakkuk 1—2
gives us an instructive example. After the heading ('The oracle
which Habakkuk the prophet saw') we hear the prophet laying
his complaint before Yahweh (1.2–4). The style is like that of the
individual psalms of lament and the 'confessions' of Jeremiah.
The first part is in the Qina rhythm (favoured for laments and
dirges). But although it is phrased as an individual's lament, we
can see from other considerations that Habakkuk speaks for the

58

community, and Yahweh's reply, as we shall see, is directed to a plurality. The prophet complains of injustice in very general language; from the book as a whole I take it he laments the condition of his people under Assyrian domination, and so around 640 or 630 B.C.:

How long, Yahweh, must I cry out
and you will not hear,
how long bewail cruelty
but you will not save?

Why do you make me see wrongs
and look upon oppression?
Yes, strife prevails
and dispute arises.

And so true guidance has grown cold
and good rule no longer shines out,
but the wicked man encircles the righteous
and the rule that goes out is crooked.

The *nabi*-prophet has thus used his gift of intercession, reaching to the heart of God with his moving poetry. He waits, and presently his gift of perceiving the response of God is active. A revelation comes to him, also in poetic form, and he speaks as God's mouthpiece (1.5–11):

Look, all of you, among the nations and see
and be astounded and astonished,
for a deed I do in your days –
if it were told you, you would not believe it!
For look, I raise up the Chaldeans,
that people fierce and swift
that traverses vast tracts of the earth
to possess the dwellings of others.
Fearsome and terrible are they,
a people independent and proud,
faster than leopards their horses,
keener than hungry wolves....

– and so the description continues of the weapon which Yahweh will unleash against the huge Assyrian empire.

We have seen how prophecies of God's warfare are sometimes duplicated, as though to strike the more effectively (p. 20; cf. Gen. 41.32). So here, the prophet doubles his complaint to Yahweh,

59

seeking for his troubled people corroboration of Yahweh's promise to bring relief (1.12–17). So once again the other side of the prophet's endowment comes into action; from powerful presentation of the weapon against the oppressor he turns now to challenging and moving intercession:

> Are you not from the very beginning, Yahweh,
> my God, my Holy One who will never die?
> Yahweh, it was for good rule you appointed him [the Assyrian]
> and as a rock of justice you founded him –
> you whose eyes are too pure to look at evil,
> you who cannot countenance oppression,
> why *do* you countenance the treacherous,
> why *are* you silent when the wicked man
> swallows up the one who is in the right?
>
> And you have made mankind to be
> like the fish of the sea,
> like crawling things that have no ruler.
> In masses he [the Assyrian] brings them up with the net,
> he scoops them up with his drag-net,
> he sweeps them up with his fish-net.
>
> And so he celebrates with joyful worship
> and sacrifices to his drag-net
> and burns incense to his fish-net,
> for through these he has got a fat portion
> and sumptuous fare.
> Shall he then for ever empty his net
> and never forbear to slay the peoples?

Having laid this further sharp and moving complaint before Yahweh, the prophet waits and watches for the reply. Fortunately he has preserved a formula describing this process of waiting (2.1–2):

> Now let me stay at my vigil
> and station myself on siege and keep watch
> to perceive what he will speak through me
> and what answer I must bring back concerning my complaint.
>
> Now Yahweh answers me and says ...

Similar phrases of prophetic vigil occur in Isaiah 21.6f., and we may also recall Psalm 85 (p. 55):

I will listen for what the God Yahweh will say [the Greek adds
'through me']
– yes, he speaks *šālōm*....

Yahweh's second answer to Habakkuk (2.2b–4) is thus:

Write down the revelation
and set it down plainly upon tablets
so that it is clear to read.
For still the revelation is for a set time,
though it pants eagerly towards the end
and will not prove false.
Though it must tarry,
wait for it
for it will surely come
and not be late.

This is all preliminary, and tension must be mounting as to what
the revelation actually is. It comes in 2.4 – and is rather
mysterious!

See, the soul of this one is puffed up, not sound within him,
but the good man through his faithfulness shall be well.

The first line is a diagnosis and implied death-sentence on the
oppressor, whom I take to be the Assyrian. Healthy and
successful outwardly he may be, but God declares him fevered
and swollen within – a condition resulting from arrogance; he
cannot live! The second line pronounces life for the righteous, the
oppressed people of God. Through their faithfulness they will
come at last to a full and healthy life.

Our next example of a prophet voicing interchanges between
God and congregation comes from Isaiah 33. Here also we find a
double pattern. The first interchange is found in verses 1–6. This
begins with announcement from God's side (v. 1); doom is
pronounced for the oppressor:

Woe to you, destroyer
who have not suffered destruction,
you treacherous one
whom no one betrayed!
When you have finished destroying
you will be destroyed,
when you have completed your treachery
they will betray you.

61

The prophet then voices the people's response in the style of a communal lament (v. 2):

> Yahweh, be gracious to us!
> For you we wait.
> Be our arm[6] every morning,
> our salvation in the time of affliction!

There follows what may be taken as an answer from the side of God, for it is a visionary depiction of God coming to the rescue:

> At the roaring sound peoples flee,
> at your thunder[7] nations scatter
> and spoil is taken
> like the taking of the locusts,
> like the leaping of locust swarms
> men leap upon it.
> Yahweh appears in majesty above all
> for his abode is in the heights.
> He fills Zion with good rule and order....

As in Habakkuk (pp. 59–60), the lamentation is renewed as though to seek corroboration (vv. 7–9):

> Behold, the ministers of God (?) wail in the court,
> those that should bring good tidings weep bitterly,
> the processional routes are in disrepair,
> no one passes along the ways!
> He [the oppressor] has broken covenants,
> rejected cities
> and despised human life.
>
> The earth mourns and withers,
> Lebanon wails and moulders,
> Sharon is turned to desert,
> Bashan and Carmel drop their leaves.

Having laid this lament before God, the prophet may have waited as Habakkuk did, 'besieging' God for an answer. Presently he is able to come back to the congregation with an oracle (v. 10f.):

> Now indeed I will arise, says Yahweh,
> Now indeed I will exalt myself,
> Now indeed I will rise for action!
>
> You [oppressors] conceive chaff,
> you give birth to stubble,

you breathe out fire only to burn yourselves,
yes, the hostile peoples will be burnings of lime,
cuttings of thorn bush set on fire.

Further revelation is given in verse 13f., applying to Zion the
message of Yahweh's advent. Rather as in Psalm 24 and Micah 6
(p. 49), there is teaching in 'tora' form about the qualities needed
in those who will be able to live in the city of God's presence:

Hear, distant ones, what I have done,
you that are near, know my power!

Sinners in Zion tremble,
Quaking seizes the impious.

Who among us can abide with the devouring fire,
who among us can abide with the eternal flames?

He who walks aright and speaks justly,
who rejects the gain of oppression,
who shakes out his hands lest they hold a bribe,
who stops his ear from talk of bloodshed,
who shuts his eyes from approving evil.

Such a one may dwell on the heights,
fastnesses of rocks shall be his fortress,
his bread provided, his water secured.

From verse 17 such promise is developed and addressed to 'you'
singular – presumably the collective people acceptable to God:

A king in his splendour your eyes shall see,
they shall see a spacious territory.
Your heart shall muse concerning the terror,
Where are the inspectors who counted and weighed,
where are the inspectors who counted the turrets?
The gesticulating people you shall see no more,
people of incomprehensible speech,
of peculiar language, impossible to understand.
Look upon Zion, city of our festival!
Your eyes shall see Jerusalem
as a peaceful abode,
a tent that will not be moved,
whose pegs will never be uprooted
and whose ropes will never be snapped.

In verse 21 the prophet voices the congregation's response, a thankful and confident hymn similar to Psalm 48, etc.:

> Yes, there Yahweh will triumph for us
> in a place of currents, wide rivers,
> where no oared ship can go
> or proud ship pass.
> Yes, Yahweh is our ruler,
> Yahweh is our governor,
> Yahweh is our King,
> It is he who will save us.

Finally there is promise again from the side of God. There is some doubt as to the reference of verse 23; is the image of a storm-battered ship applied to the oppressor, or to the suffering of Zion now to be remedied? Or could it be the image of a tent that can scarcely accommodate so large a family (Zion, as in 54.2)?

> Your cords are loosened
> till they scarcely hold upright their pole
> or keep the pennant flying.

> Then spoil in plenty will be shared,
> even the lame share the plunder
> and no inhabitant will say, I am sick,
> the city's population will be pardoned from sin.

In Isaiah 33 the alternation of speech on behalf of God and of the congregation is so fluid that some commentators consider it a very late passage (Hellenistic, according to Kaiser) where an apocalyptic poet loosely uses the old forms of dialogue. But we might rather see its character as due not to remoteness from the original practice of such dialogue, but to the very nature of those interchanges which could pass through the one man in his twin roles of intercessor and seer. It is not surprising that sometimes these roles tended to intermingle and produce such material as Isaiah 33.

Another example of the dialogue is provided by Isaiah 59. Although the first speech is from the side of God, it has the character of a rejoinder to lament from the side of the people about the failure of salvation to materialize – as though they had said: 'Has Yahweh's hand become too short?', etc. To such laments the prophet can now state on God's behalf that there is nothing amiss with Yahweh's hand or ear; the impediment is his

people's wickedness by which their hands and lips are defiled
(vv. 1–4):

> Look, the hand of Yahweh is not too short to save,
> his ear is not too thick to hear,
> but your iniquities make a barrier between you and your God
> for your palms are defiled with blood
> and your fingers with iniquity,
> your lips speak falsehood,
> your tongue mutters wickedness.
>
> There is no one going to law justly,
> no one contending in the courts honestly.
> You trust in empty talk and speak falsehood,
> you are pregnant with oppression
> and give birth to evil.

Accusation continues in a second unit (vv. 5–8), which may be
directed at a particular group of the people, 'they':

> They hatch adder's eggs,
> they weave spider's webs.
> He who tastes their eggs dies
> and from the broken egg is hatched a viper.
>
> Their webs will not make a garment,
> what they weave will give no warmth,
> their products are only evil,
> their hands make only oppression,
> their feet run to do evil
> and they hasten to shed innocent blood.
> Their plans are plans for iniquity,
> plunder and destruction mark their road,
> the way of peace they do not know,
> there is no justice in their paths,
> their tracks are crooked,
> none who treads in them knows peace.

Now follows the community's response to these harsh criticisms
(59.9–15), led, we may suppose, by the prophet in intercessory
role, with lamentation and confession of sin:

> Truly, good order is far from us
> and salvation does not arrive for us.
> We wait for light, and look, darkness!
> We wait for dawn, but we must walk in black night,

we grope for the wall like blind men,
we stumble at midday as if at nightfall,
among the living we fall like dead men.
All of us groan like bears,
we moan and moan like doves.
We wait for your good rule
but it does not come,
and for salvation
but it is still far from us.
For our offences are many in your sight
and our sins witness against us,
yes, our offences are still with us
and our sins we do acknowledge.
There has been rebellion and lying against Yahweh,
turning back from following our God,
speaking oppression and revolt,
conceiving and uttering in the heart words of falsehood,
and good rule is repelled
and right order stands far off,
yes, truth has fallen in the square
and uprightness cannot enter
and faithfulness is not to be found
and integrity has been plundered away.

The mournful tones of the lament die away. In the deep silence of
the prophet's soul there comes at last the conviction that Yahweh
is moved by the penitence and pleading. He sees God coming
with power to save and he reports accordingly. The good news is
expressed in vivid poetry, as though to give impetus to the work
of salvation (59.15b–20):

Yahweh has seen and is indignant that there is no good rule
and he has seen that none comes to help
and is astonished that none intervenes,
so his own arm brings salvation
and his own right order is his support,
he has put on right order as his breastplate
and salvation is the helmet on his head
and he wears vengeance as his clothing
and wraps himself in zeal for a cloak.
Full requital he will render,
wrath to his foes, recompense to his enemies,
to farthest coastlands he will deal recompense
that they may fear the name of Yahweh where the sun sets,

and his glory where it rises.
For he comes like a fierce river
which the wind of Yahweh drives,
and he comes to Zion as redeemer
and to the penitents in Jacob
– utterance of Yahweh.

A related sequence of dialogue, considered to be substantially from the exilic period,[8] is found in Isaiah 63—5. As in Psalm 82 (pp. 57–8), the starting-point is a dramatic vision of Yahweh punishing oppressors. The blood-stained God enters in triumph and tells at the gate of the war he has waged to redeem his oppressed people (p. 31). The message is thus that help is indeed on the way, though not yet visible to ordinary sight. Also, as in Psalm 82, the report of the visionary scene (63.1–6) is followed by response on behalf of the congregation (63.7—64.12). Here it flows at length, very much in the style of the psalms of communal lament and constituting an appeal that the promised intervention may materialize. To this end it recalls Yahweh's past interventions, portrays present distress, and makes confession of sin:

I will recount how Yahweh kept his promises of old,
the praises of Yahweh ...
you led your people
to make for yourself a glorious name.

Look from heaven and see
from your holy and beautiful dwelling!
Where now your zeal and mighty deeds?
The tumult of your compassion and love
is withheld from me.
But you are our father
though Abraham should not know us
or Israel recognize us,
you, Yahweh, are our father,
from earliest times your name is Our Redeemer.
Why, Yahweh, did you make us wander from your ways,
why did you harden our heart so as not to fear you?
Return, for the sake of your servants,
the tribes of your inheritance!
For a little while your holy people had possession.
Now our enemies have trampled your sanctuary,

we have long been as though not ruled by you,
as though not called by your name.
If only you would tear apart heaven and descend
and the mountains quake before you!

We have all become like something defiled
and all our endeavours have become like a polluted garment
and we have all faded like a leaf
and our iniquities carry us away like the wind.

The lament further states that no minister seems capable of
effective prayer, none is enabled by Yahweh to make the
immense effort (64.6/7):

And there is none who can invoke your name,
stirring himself up to lay hold upon you,
for you have hidden your face from us
and given us[9] into the power of our sins.

But come now, Yahweh, you are our father,
we were the clay, you the one who moulded us,
we are all the work of your hand.

The appeal resembles Psalm 74 as the ruin of the temple, etc. is
movingly depicted (64.8/9f.):

Do not be angry to excess, Yahweh,
do not for ever remember iniquity!
Come now, see – we are your people,
your holy cities have become a wilderness,
Zion has become a wilderness,
Jerusalem a desolation,
our holy and beautiful temple where our fathers praised you
has been burned down
and all our lovely places have been ruined.
For all these things will you hold aloof, Yahweh,
will you stay silent and afflict us to excess?

The earnestly sought answer of God may be found in Isaiah 65.
Even if those commentators are right who consider that it reflects
a different situation, it is significant that the arranger of this
material recognized the appropriate pattern by placing here such
an oracle. Yahweh is thus shown to reject any charge of slowness
to hear, etc. – on the contrary, he had come and found none ready
for him. It was he who spread out his hand imploringly and his

people who ignored him, devoted as they were to their sinful deeds. So the chapters maintain the tradition of spirited dialogue, each party giving as good as he gets.

The prophets' struggle to assuage God's wrath

As we follow further the interchanges of God and people articulated by the ministries of prophets, we now come to see more closely the work of a prophet when he had to announce the threats of an angry God but also had to put himself in the path of that wrath to turn it aside.

While all intercession was exacting, often carried out with fasting, lying on the ground, and for long periods (cf. Deut. 9.18f.; Josh. 7; 1 Sam. 15.11), it was considered to be a terrible and dangerous work to stand in the way of deity aroused. Now it was seen that to 'draw near' as intercessor before Yahweh was to give one's heart as pledge ('āzab; Jer. 30.21), offering it to be forfeit, ready to surrender one's life. Only the true prophet stood at his post, shielding the people, when the divine wrath welled up. Ezekiel tells of shallow prophets who, when the attacking God breached his people's defences, failed to move into the gap and raise a barrier of intercession, fleeing instead like foxes startled in the desert (Ezek. 13.4–5; 22.30). The ideal is expressed in several stories of Moses, who offered his own life as he blocked the way of God's own anger (cf. Ps. 106.23), who was once told by God, 'Out of my way, that my anger may blaze upon them and I may put an end to them' (Exod. 32.10f.), and who in the end died short of the promised land for his people's sake (Deut. 1.37; 3.23f.; 4.21f.).

It is in the light of this ideal of prophetic duty that we can better appreciate the persistent efforts of prophets like Amos or Jeremiah to deflect the approaching wrath they saw so vividly.

First we consider a remarkable sequence in Jeremiah 14— 15.9. While some think that the sequence has been developed by later expansion, Reventlow has argued that the whole can be accepted as a continuous transaction in worship. At all events, if we follow the material as it stands, we shall be following Jeremiah's experience either directly, or through the eyes of his successors, who knew a lot about Jeremiah and the customs of prophecy and worship.

We see the prophet mediating in a crisis brought about by drought. His work in leading the lamentation and speaking for God is indirectly compared to that of Moses and Samuel when Yahweh says, 'Though Moses and Samuel stood before me, yet my heart would not turn towards this people. Send them out of my sight....' (Jer. 15.1). Thus the people are assembled at the temple, and Jeremiah's part has called to mind that of Samuel (1 Sam. 7.5f.), when the people assembled before Yahweh at Mizpah and drew and poured out water before Yahweh and fasted and confessed their sin while Samuel prayed to Yahweh incessantly with sacrifice (cf. Jer. 14.12). The approach is first from the side of the afflicted people, and the prophet accordingly voices a lament to move Yahweh by depiction of the sufferings (14.2-6):

Judah mourns
and her gates pine.
They lament on the ground
and the wailing of Jerusalem goes up.
Their nobles have sent their servants for water,
they came to the cisterns,
found no water,
returned with their vessels empty,
they are ashamed and confounded
and cover their heads.
On account of the ground,
cracked for lack of the winter rain,
the ploughmen are ashamed,
they cover their heads.

Even the hind in the wild
gives birth and forsakes her calf
because there is no herbage.
The wild asses stand on the heights,
they snuff the wind like jackals,
their eyes search in vain for grass.

The appeal to Yahweh now becomes more direct, with stress on penitence and on the bond with Yahweh their Saviour. The communal 'we' is used (14.7-10) and the style is very rhythmic and resonant:

Though our misdeeds witness against us,
Yahweh, act for the sake of your name!

Yes, our defections have been many,
against you we have sinned.

You hope of Israel,
his saviour in time of distress,
why should you be like an alien in the land,
like a traveller who lodges overnight?

Then, even more provocatively (14.9):

Why should you be like someone stunned,
like a champion who cannot save?
And you are the God in our midst,
yours is the name called over us –
do not throw us off!

The appeal has reached its climax. Now the prophet waits and watches (cf. p. 59) until he can discern Yahweh's response (14.10):

Thus says Yahweh concerning this community:
As they have loved to wander
and not held back their feet,
so Yahweh has not accepted them,
he still remembers their iniquity
and takes account of their sins.

This brief and general statement, then, is an example of a negative result. Yahweh refuses to accept the offerings and entreaties of the worshippers. Atonement, reconciliation, on this occasion has not been effected.

But the devoted intercessor would not give up so easily, and there follows a record of his wrestling with God on the people's behalf. A renewed congregational lament will be offered in verse 19f. But the intervening section, verses 11–18, shows the prophet wrestling more intimately with Yahweh and raising the question of those prophets who gave a different message. Jeremiah meets a very adamant Yahweh (v. 11):

Further, Yahweh said to me:
Do not intercede for the salvation of this people!
Though they are fasting
I refuse to hear their cries,
though they are offering whole-offering and cereal gifts
I refuse to accept them,
but by sword, famine and pestilence
I will destroy them.

71

Thus Yahweh not only refuses to lift the drought, but threatens all the other curses traditionally allotted for covenant-breaking. But the prophet dares still to counter in his role of intercessor; with tactful obliqueness he implies that the blame lies on irresponsible prophets rather than on the people (14.13):

And I said,
Alas, Lord Yahweh!
See, the prophets are saying to them,
You will not see the sword,
you will not have famine,
but I will give you real prosperity from this sanctuary.

Yahweh's response is unremitting (14.14f.):

Falsehood such prophets prophesy in my name,
I have not sent them nor commanded them
nor spoken to them.
A false vision, worthless divination
and deceit of their own heart
they prophesy to you ...
and I will pour upon them their iniquity –
so you must say to them.

After this stern revelation the prophet raises a lament for his people (14.17bf.). We notice that he now refers to effects of warfare as well as of famine. Reventlow suggests that Jeremiah is countering the potential reality launched by the preceding oracle rather than depicting actual circumstances; but perhaps we simply have impressions of general anarchy. Jeremiah here speaks of an unceasing work of lamentation, and we recall how Samuel (1 Sam. 12.23) considered that if he ceased interceding for the people it would be a heinous sin; thus Jeremiah:

Let my eyes run down with tears night and day
and let them not cease,
for with a great breaking she is broken,
she, my dear one, my people,
with a very grave wounding.

If I go out into the open land,
look, people fallen by the sword,
and if I enter the city,
look, people faint with famine!
For prophet and priest alike
have trafficked[10] ignorantly.

The intercession now becomes a typical communal lament, returning to the basic concern with the drought (14.19f.):

Have you completely rejected Judah
or does your soul now loathe Zion?
Why have you beaten us
and allowed us no healing?
Why did we hope for health
but found no favour for healing? –
and look, nothing but terror!

We acknowledge, Yahweh, our wickedness,
the iniquity of our fathers –
we have all sinned against you.
For your name's sake do not spurn us,
do not despise the throne of your glory,
recall and do not annul your covenant with us!

Are there powers to bring rain
among the vain gods of the nations?
Or can the heavens themselves give showers?
Are you not the only one, Yahweh our God?
And we will hope only for you
for you alone have made all these things.

And so to the waiting and the watching, and at length the prophet's perception – a God still adamant, still thoroughly displeased with the lives of his people! Jeremiah bears back a heavy message; the full range of the curses on covenant-breakers is to be applied (15.1–4):

Then Yahweh said to me:
Though it were Moses and Samuel interceding before me
my soul would not turn to this people.
Dismiss them from my presence and let them depart
and if they say to you, Where shall we go?
then say to them,
Thus says Yahweh –
those who are for death, to death,
those who are for the sword, to the sword,
those who are for famine, to famine
and those who are for captivity, to captivity!

And I commission for them four species
– so the utterance of Yahweh –
sword to slay,

    dogs to drag away,
    birds of the skies,
    beasts of the land
    to devour and destroy....[11]

In 15.5 we hear an elegiac lament over the fallen. This is hardly a
resumption of intercessory lament, overtaken in verse 6 by
renewed oracles of doom (Reventlow); it is rather the anticipatory
dirge which confirms the coming death (p. 23):

    Oh, who will have pity on you, Jerusalem?
    Oh, who will show sympathy for you,
    or who will turn aside to ask after your health?

And so to the conclusion, oracles of doom (15.6–9):

    You, you have forsaken me
    – it is Yahweh's oracle –
    away from me you have gone
    and so I stretch my hand against you and destroy you
    for I am weary of relenting....

Valuable insights into the setting of the prophetic struggles to
avert the wrath of God are afforded by the Book of Joel, which
may be dated before the Exile or shortly after. The community, it
appears, is suffering from a plague of locusts. Joel's first words
are not appeals directed to God, but calls to the community to
gather in fasting and prayer at the temple. But these calls from
God's messenger are filled out with depictions of the affliction in
the style of the laments (cf. p. 70). The effect is to inaugurate the
penitential rites, setting the mood for the people's penitence.

At the outset, then (1.2f.), we hear the man from God jolting
the people into full awareness of the affliction and summoning
them to the penitential ceremonies:

    Hear this, elders,
    listen, all inhabitants of the land!
    Has such a thing happened in your days
    or in the days of your fathers?
    You will tell your children about it
    and your children will tell their children
    and their children their successors.

    Whatever the cutting locusts leave
    the swarming locusts eat
    and what the swarming locusts leave

the hopping locusts eat
and what the hopping locusts leave
the locust grubs eat up.

Wake up, you drunkards and weep,
wail, all you tipplers of wine,
wail for the sweet wine
for it is cut off from your mouth!

For a horde has attacked my land,
mighty and beyond counting,
with teeth like teeth of lions
and fangs of a lioness.

It has ruined my vines
and wrecked my fig trees,
stripping them
and leaving branches broken and white.

Lament [dear one][12] like a virgin wife
girded with sackcloth
over the husband she married so young!

Gifts of cereals and drink are cut off
from the house of Yahweh.
The priests mourn,
those who served Yahweh.

The open land is desolate,
the ground mourns,
yes, the corn is desolate,
the new wine grieves,
the oil mourns.

Mourn, tillers of the soil,
wail, fruit growers
over the wheat and barley
for the harvest of the field is lost.

The vine grieves,
and the fig tree mourns,
pomegranates, palm, and apple —
all the trees of the field are withered,
yes, rejoicing has ceased from mankind.

Gird for mourning, priests,
wail, you that served the altar,
enter and lie all night in sackcloth,

you that served my God,
for offerings of cereal and drink
are withheld from the house of your God.

Proclaim a fast,
call a solemn assembly,
gather the elders and all inhabitants of the land
in the house of Yahweh your God
and cry out to Yahweh!

Ah, that day!
Yes, the day of Yahweh is very near
and comes as doom from the Almighty.

The decisive, ultimate action of Yahweh, foreshadowed by his festal advents, is here apprehended as hostile to this people (cf. p. 32). At this point (1.16f.) the lamenting element is turned back to God as a cry on the people's behalf, a further illustration of the easy switch of roles in the one person of the prophet (cf. p. 64):

Is not the food cut off before our very eyes,
joy and celebration from the house of our God? ...

The stores are desolate,
the granaries are ruinous
for the corn has failed.
How the beasts groan,
the herds of cattle suffer
for they have no pasture!
The flocks also are dismayed.

The prophet exerts himself all the more directly now as intercessor (1.19f.):

To you I cry, Yahweh,
for fire has eaten the pastures of the wilderness
and flames have consumed all the trees of the open land,
even the wild beasts look up to you panting
for the channels of water are dried up
and fire has eaten the pastures of the wilderness.

Is reference made here to an additional trouble, forest fires after the long summer drought and the devastating locusts?

The prophet now speaks again from God's side (2.1f.) in that he warns the people of worse to come, a cataclysm of Yahweh's wrath, and so urges them to make penance before it is too late.

The horns that call the people to the fast are like alarms that warn
of approaching attack:

> Blow the ram's-horn in Zion,
> sound the alarm on my holy mountain!
> Let all the inhabitants of the land tremble
> for the day of Yahweh comes,
> yes, it is very near,
> day of darkness and blackness,
> day of cloud and thick darkness,
> like a blackness spread over the mountains!
> A host numerous and mighty –
> the like of it never was
> and never shall be for all time to come.

Through the locusts and fires of the present affliction the prophet
is seeing a vision of greater wrath, the day of Yahweh and his
avenging armies, with a dire threat to the prophet's community.
So Joel depicts his visionary terrors with eloquence to induce
repentance:

> Before them burns fire
> and after them licks the flame,
> before them – land like the garden of Eden,
> after them – a desolate wilderness
> and nothing escapes them.

> They look like war-horses,
> they run like cavalry,
> with a din like chariots
> they leap the tops of the mountains,
> with a din like flames devouring stubble,
> like a mighty army in lines for battle.

> Before them peoples writhe,
> faces turn purple with anguish.
> Like warriors they run,
> like shock troops they scale walls,
> each keeps to his track,
> they do not yield their paths,
> none jostles his fellow,
> each keeps to his line,
> through missiles they charge
> and are not checked,
> they leap upon the city,

they run along the wall,
they go up into the houses,
through the windows they enter like thieves,
before them the land trembles,
the heavens quake,
sun and moon are darkened
and the stars lose their brightness.

It is Yahweh who utters his voice before his host,
yes, vast is his army,
countless those who obey his command.
Yes, great is the day of Yahweh and very terrible
and who can endure it?

Yet even now – it is Yahweh's utterance –
return to me with all your heart
and with fasting and weeping and mourning,
tear your hearts rather than your clothes
and return to Yahweh your God,
for he is gracious and compassionate,
long-suffering and ever faithful
and ready to relent from destruction.
Who knows if he may now relent again
and leave behind him blessing,
[restoring] the offerings of grain and drink
for Yahweh your God?

The call for the fast now grows more urgent and the supplication
of a lament is begun (2.15f.):

Blow the ram's-horn in Zion,
appoint a fast,
call a solemn assembly,
gather the people,
convoke the assembly,
gather the elders,
gather the children,
even those still at the breast,
let the bridegroom come from his room
and the bride from her bower!

Between the temple-porch and the altar [in the court]
let the priests weep,
those who served Yahweh,
and let them say:

Have pity on your people, Yahweh
and give not your heritage over to taunts
and to the dominance of the nations!
Why should they say among the nations,
Where is your God?

Thus the prophet has delivered his dire warning and given
momentum to the penitential rites which may avert God's wrath.
As all the population, from the elderly to the infants, come
together, a dishevelled and weeping choir of priests take up the
burden of the lament the prophet has commenced for them. The
record of Joel's work then tells us of the outcome of the
penitential rites. Unlike Jeremiah, Joel can bring a good response
from God (2.18f.):

Then Yahweh burned with zeal for his land
and took pity on his people
and Yahweh answered and said to his people,

Look, I send you corn and wine and oil
and you will have your fill of them
and I will not make you an object of mockery among nations
and the peril from the north I will remove far from you
and drive it away into a land of desert and desolation,
its vanguard into the eastern sea
and its rearguard into the western sea –
its stench will rise and smell of rot go up
for it exceeded its task.

The prophecy of good continues with elements of hymnic
celebration:

Fear not, O soil,
celebrate and rejoice,
for it is Yahweh who has done great things!
Fear not, wild beasts,
for the pastures of the wilderness will be green,
yes, the trees will bear their fruit
and the figs and vines will yield richly.

And you, sons of Zion,
celebrate and rejoice in Yahweh your God
for he will give you the early rain as it should be
and send down for you the winter rain,
early and latter rain as of old,

79

and the threshing-floors will be full of corn
and the vats shall overflow with wine and oil
and I will make good for you the years
which the locusts have eaten,
the hopping locusts,
the grubs and the cutting locusts,
my great host which I sent among you,
and you shall eat your fill
and praise the name of Yahweh your God
for the miracles he has done for you
and my people shall never be put to shame
and you shall know that I am in the midst of Israel
and I am Yahweh your God and there is no other
and my people shall never be ashamed.

This favourable message is then developed from 2.30–32 and further again in chapters 3 and (Hebrew) 4. The terrible day of Yahweh will deal with enemies of God's people, but all who call on his name will be delivered. Restoration will take place for Jerusalem (the old formula of thorough renewal, p. 34) and judgement will be executed on the nations in the valley of Jehoshaphat (= 'Yahweh judges'). The judgement will be like a harvest and the pressing of grapes – 'multitudes, multitudes in the valley of decision'. The prophecies culminate with ever greater emphasis on Zion. There Yahweh appears and roars (cf. p. 37). From his temple a fountain will flow and the mountain land will become wonderfully fertile.

Joel gives us a valuable clue as to the juxtaposition of threats and promises, often so abrupt in the prophets. For in Joel the transition is clearly explained. Threats were uttered, penitence followed with the doom-prophet now active in intercession, and so eventually came a change of message – restoration for true worshippers and unfolding of miraculous prospects. Joel is thus evidence that we should not divide prophets into doom and šālōm prophets. Joel was ready to speak either as appropriate and the two aspects of his work revolve around his role as sentinel and intercessor. We may compare Ezekiel, set as a lookout for Israel; he might have to say to a man, 'Wicked one, you shall surely die!' – but in the hope that repentance would avert the sentence (Ezek. 33.7–9).

Another fruitful text for our inquiry is Micah 7. Verses 1–7 are a lament in individual form by the prophet, and intended for the hearing of God. He depicts the faults of the society in a way which might have been turned against the people as a condemnation from God, but here it is directed to God to move him to rectify things. Perhaps this amounts to a kind of confession on behalf of society (cf. below, v. 9). Briefly, in verse 4b, the prophet touches on his other role, reflecting the judgement of God, and here comparison can be made with the communal laments of Psalms 12 and 14 which also bemoan the corruption of society and convey the judgement of God. Micah, as Jeremiah often does, here places his own person as intercessor to the fore:

> *'al^elay lī* Ah me!
> I have become
> as when the summer fruit has been gathered in,
> as when the vintage has been gleaned
> and there is no cluster to eat,
> no first-ripe fig for which I crave.
>
> The faithful have vanished from earth
> and there is no upright person among mankind.
> They all lie in wait to shed blood
> and each hunts his brother with a net,
> their hands are diligent to do evil,
> officials and judges ask for bribes...
> (4b) the day of your sentinels,[13]
> your visitation has come,
> now confusion shall fall on them!
>
> Put no trust in your fellow,
> have no confidence in a friend,
> guard the doors of your mouth
> from her who lies in your bosom
> for the son treats the father with contempt,
> the daughter rises up against her mother,
> the daughter-in-law against her mother-in-law –
> a man's enemies are his own family.
>
> But for my part I will keep watch for Yahweh,
> I will wait for the God pledged to my salvation –
> may my God hear me!

The continuation is in the style of the 'confidence' section of an individual lament. Now it is clearer that the individual speaker is representative of the community and acknowledges sin. There is

81

sharp rebuttal of enemies in the form of a female personification, denoting another nation such as Edom or Assyria, and the following answer from God is addressed to a feminine singular (Zion):

> Do not exult over me, woman that hates me!
> Though I fall, I shall rise again,
> though I dwell in darkness, Yahweh will be my light.
> (v. 9) I must bear the indignation of Yahweh
> because I have sinned against him
> until he takes up my cause
> and secures justice for me.
> He will bring me out into the light,
> I shall enjoy his deliverance,
> then she that hates me will see
> and shame will cover her
> who said to me, Where is Yahweh your God?
> My eyes will relish her downfall,
> now she will be trampled
> like the mire of the streets.

From verse 11 we hear speech of oracular character to a feminine singular (Zion):

> A day for the building of your walls!
> In that day the boundary shall be far extended,
> in that day they will come to you[14]
> from Assyria and the cities of Egypt
> and from Egypt to the Euphrates,
> from every sea and every mountain
> and the earth shall become waste because of its inhabitants,
> for the fruit of their doings.

Response is then made to God's promise in the style of the appeal in communal laments (v. 14f.):

> Shepherd your people with your staff,
> the flock of your possession
> which dwells alone in woodland, in the midst of Carmel,
> let them feed in Bashan and Gilead as in the days of old,
> As in the days when you came out of Egypt
> show us miracles!

The conclusion (vv. 18–20) is an expression of confidence such as might round off a psalm of communal lament:

Who is a God like you
pardoning iniquity and passing over transgression
for the remnant of the people he owns?
He does not hold his anger for ever
for his pleasure is in the bonds of love,
he will again have compassion on us,
he will trample on our iniquities –
yes, you will cast all their sins into the depths of the sea,
you will deal truly with Jacob
and keep faith with Abraham
as you swore to our fathers from the days of old.

Thus in Micah 7 the central body is a dialogue in verses 8–20 of community and God, with the community speaking partly as a feminine singular and partly as first person plural. The preceding section (vv. 1–7) appears more 'personal' to the individual prophet but may well be an intended preliminary to the main dialogue. The prophet's lament before God in verses 1–7 asks God's help over the bad state of society, but also prepares the people to repent. He can then voice the people's contrition and confidence of help (8–10), then bring back the promise of God (11–13), then lead the community's response with psalmic elements of appeal and confidence (14–20). The chapter thus gives us further illustration of a ministry which began with keen recognition of the sins of the society and then strove to avert the visitation of divine wrath and achieve reconciliation of God and people.

Further examples of such a ministry can be found in the Book of Hosea. Within the sequence 5.8—7.16 we may concentrate on 5.15—6.6. First the prophet expresses Yahweh's voice, inviting repentance:

I will go again to my sanctuary
until they know their guilt and seek my face,
until in their distress they eagerly seek me.

Next (6.1–3) there comes in response expression of the people's repentance and trust in Yahweh's power to heal. Although commentators are inclined to dissociate Hosea from this utterance, we can well take it that he here continues his prophetic ministry by leading the people before God. It is true that not much is said here explicitly of confession of guilt, but in traditional liturgical utterance one item is implicit in another. There is a clear desire for turning to Yahweh and a beautiful expression of faith in his grace. Several words[15] echo the preceding speeches of Yahweh, making it the more likely that the dialogue passes both ways through Hosea:

> Come, let us turn again to Yahweh!
> Though he has torn, yet can he heal us,
> though he has struck, yet will he dress our wounds,
> he can revive us after two days,
> on the third day he will raise us up
> that we may have life in his presence and know him –
> yes, let us seek to know Yahweh!
> Faithful as the dawn is his rising
> and he will come to us like the rain,
> as the showers that moisten the earth.

Hosea will then have waited and watched (p. 60) and eventually he brings back from God an answer which is not outright acceptance or rejection. It is a word with tones of love and yearning, and yet it must point realistically to the obstacles to reconciliation. Yahweh does not criticize the preceding words of repentance and faith, but complains of a national life which does not keep to the standards of the covenant. They may give their pledge, but will they honour it?

> What should I do to you, Ephraim,
> what should I do to you, Judah?
> Your fidelity is like the morning mist,
> like the dew that vanishes early.
> This is why I hewed with the prophets
> and slew with the words of my mouth
> and judgements went out against you at dawn.
> Fidelity I want, not sacrifice,
> knowledge of God rather than burnt offerings.

Now in Hosea 14 there is further dialogue, and here the tremendous divine urge for reconciliation prevails over all obstacles. As in Joel (p. 74), the prophet issues a summons to repentance before turning again to God to voice the people's prayer and hope (Hos. 14.2/1):

Turn again, Israel, to Yahweh your God!
Though you have stumbled in your iniquity
take with you words
and turn again to Yahweh!

Say to him:
Forgive, we pray, all iniquity,
accept us favourably
and we will pay the fruit of our lips![16]
Assyria cannot save us,
we will not ride on horses
and we will not again say 'our God'
to what we have made with our hands.
In you the fatherless will find compassion.

Hosea is then able to give Yahweh's rejoinder, a word of
acceptance, promising healing and life in the rich language of
natural growth and fertility, indeed with the tones of a love-song.
The indirect style ('they', 'them') indicates how the word is given
to the intercessor, which he has then to report (14.5/4):

I heal their infidelity,
I love them abundantly,
yes, my anger has turned back from him,
I will be like dew to Israel,
he will flower like a lily,
strike root as on Lebanon,
his shoots will spread,
his splendour shall be like the olive's
and he shall have fragrance like that of Lebanon.

Inhabitants will gather under his shade,
again they shall grow corn,
they shall bud as the vine
and be famed as the wine of Lebanon.

Then a final direct, appealing word from God to his people
(14.9/8):

O Ephraim, enough of idols!
I myself have answered
and will watch over my promise.
I am like a green juniper,
from me you will gather fruit.

Further traces of dialogue

The dialogue of worship should also be borne in mind in a number of important passages where the people's side is not preserved, but happens to be indicated by an echo of it in the divine answer. Several examples in Isaiah 40—55 have led commentators to conclude that much of the material is divine response to congregational lament (p. 28). For example, in 40.27 the prophet makes it clear that he is answering just such a traditional lament:

Why, Jacob, do you say,
why, Israel, do you speak so,
My way is hidden from Yahweh
and my case goes unheeded by my God?

The following verses (28–31) are an answer to this lament, although argued in the prophet's own person; some even consider[17] that the whole argument of 40.12–31 is a response to this lament.

Or again, in 41.14–16, an oracle of salvation seems to presuppose a lament which had used such expressions as 'I am a worm'.[18] So the answer comes:

Do not fear, you worm Jacob....
See, I make you into a threshing sledge –
sharp, new, with many teeth.

Another example is 49.14–26, where Yahweh's words to the cultic community Zion answer her lament, from which he cites at the outset:

But Zion has said,
Yahweh has forsaken me,
The Lord has abandoned me.

God's answer is in the rhetorical, persuasive style of a truly lively dialogue:

Does a woman ever forget her baby
and not show tenderness to the son of her womb? –

And when these forget
I will not forget you.

Even when there is no obvious citation from a presupposed

lament, God's words may well be answers to such. This has been thought to be the case in Isaiah 50, where Yahweh speaks argumentatively, as if disputing and rebutting complaints[19] made on behalf of the congregation:

> Thus says Yahweh:
> Where then *is* your mother's bill of divorce
> with which I sent her away,
> and to which of my creditors did I sell you...?

A famous passage in Ezekiel (37.1–14) is illumined by consideration of such dialogue. Here also, as in Isaiah 40f., the evidence indicates that even in the Exile the people assembled and communed with God in some of the traditional words and procedures. The inspiration of Ezekiel was sometimes given to provide an answer to supplications on behalf of the congregation. In Ezekiel 37 we are fortunate that there is a representative citation from the presupposed lament, verse 11:

> They [the house of Israel] have been saying,
> Our bones are dried up
> and our hope is perished
> and we have been cut down once and for all.

With such pitiful lamentation echoing in his brain, Ezekiel, the prophet from the inner priesthood, fell into a rapture. The hand of Yahweh fell upon him. It seemed to him that the wind of God bore him up through the air to a great plain on which the people of Israel lay dead – in the form of heaps of bones, dried up, drained of all vitality. The divine wind bore him over the scene, and as he floated round and round over the heaps of bones, he launched into that place of utter hopelessness the power-filled prophecy:

> O dry bones, hear the word of Yahweh!
> See, I blow breath into you
> and you shall live again!

And so on, as in his trance he mediates for God the words that reverse the way of death into a return to life. His mind is then released from the visionary grasp, and to the waiting congregation he is able to give Yahweh's answer of hope (vv. 12–14):

87

I will open your graves ...
you shall live again
and I will place you in your own land....

A peculiar form of the dialogue of God and congregation is preserved in the Book of Malachi. Perhaps from *c.* 490 B.C., this little collection is built from six instances of such dialogue. The pattern is fairly constant. The prophet tells of a statement by God, and then of the people's objection to it, all as he addresses the people. Then he gives God's more detailed rejoinder to the objection, culminating in a final strong statement of God's position. These four elements can be traced thus in Malachi 1.2–5:

1 Yahweh says: I love you.
2 But you say: In what way do you love us?
3 Utterance of Yahweh: Is not Esau....
4 You will say, Great is Yahweh beyond Israel's border.

In the next example, 1.6—2.9, the priests make a second objection, so there are now six elements:

1 Yahweh says: A son honours his father ... where is my honour, you priests who despise my name?
2 You say: In what way do we despise your name?
3 [Yahweh:] By offering polluted food on my altar.
4 You say: In what way do we pollute it?
5 [Yahweh:] By thinking Yahweh's table may be despised....
6 And now, you priests, this decision I have made for you....

The other four examples follow in 2.10–16; 2.17—3.5; 3.6–12; 3.13–21 (English 3.13—4.3).

So in Malachi we do not have the ministry of threat–intercession–answer, or of lament–answer, but rather a situation where the prophet has announced briefly a word of God and has been countered by words from some other representatives of the people, perhaps elders or priests. Such querying of the divine announcement would not be intended quite as truculently as it sounds in the present brief citations, but would be the traditional form for eliciting the necessary details of the divine will. Malachi's pieces certainly add to what we have already seen of the experience of encounter and dialogue, God confronting an assembly, and – thanks to the prophetic offices – a lively discussion ensuing between the heavenly and earthly parties.

4 Visions of Davidic Rule

Prophetic words at enthronements in the psalms

There is another important setting of prophetic ministry in worship: the rites of the Davidic king's initiation or renewal. Such rites[1] were probably enacted in the autumn festival and showed how the reign of Yahweh, which was celebrated there, took effect through his chosen servant of David's line. The historical books already prepare us for the prominence of prophets in rites of royal initiation (1 Sam. 10.1; 1 Kings 1.34) or renewal (1 Sam. 11.14–15). The psalms show further how the authorization and empowering of the king required oracular blessing as well as sacramental rites.

The clearest example is Psalm 110. A prophetic minister delivers to the king oracles which place him close to God in the glory and victory of God's kingdom. The minister begins with the phrase commonly found in the prophetic books to signal a pronouncement of God:

> $n^{e'}\bar{u}m\ yahwe$: An utterance of Yahweh for my lord!

Yahweh's words in the first person follow:

> Sit at my right hand
> while I make your enemies
> a footstool for your feet.

Then follow words of similar effect, but with God in third person – it seems that the minister here has authority further to unfold the divine blessing upon the king:

> Yahweh extends the rod of your power from Zion!
> Prevail in the midst of your enemies!

A descriptive passage now fills the rites of anointing or lustration with meaning:

> With you is royal grace
> on this day of your birth,
> a holy apparition from the womb of dawn!
> On you is the dew of your fresh life.[2]

In verse 4 a formula is used to indicate a fundamental grant of God, one which lies in the foundations of his work with his world:

Yahweh has sworn and will not change his mind.

What follows is probably conveyance of Yahweh's own words. He bestows a royal priesthood like that of the pre-Israelite king of Jerusalem:

You are for ever a priest
of the order of Melchizedek.

As before, the minister then authoritatively unfolds the blessing, referring to God in third person. Again it seems that his words fill out the meaning of ritual acts that denote power for victory:

The Lord upon your right hand
crushes kings on the day of his anger,
he executes judgement on the nations,
making many corpses,
he smites through heads across the wide earth.

The concluding words may signify that as the Davidic king has drunk a sacramental drink, God raises his head for triumph:

From the brook by the way he drinks –
therefore he will raise his head.

Direct speech of Yahweh conveying victorious destiny to the king is found also in Psalm 132, along with blessing for the people, though with a balancing condition as often in the oracular psalms (v. 12: 'If your sons keep my covenant and my testimonies....'). After the classic statement of Yahweh's choice of the dynasty and of Zion (vv. 11–14), the oracle depicts Yahweh's blessings with rich words, creative words we might say:

Her [Zion's] provision I will bountifully bless,
Her humble ones I will feed to the full
and her priests I will dress in salvation
and her covenanters will shout in triumph.
There I will make to sprout a horn for David,
I will tend a lamp for my anointed,
his foes I will dress in defeat
while on him the flower of his headpiece will sparkle.

90

An interesting variation of form in the portrayal of prosperity for the king is offered by Psalm 72, apparently from rites of enthronement. Here the 'creative' words are not an oracle nor the further unfolding of an oracle, but at the outset a prayer which gradually takes on the force of a blessing. Just as the prophetic office included speech to God as well as speech from God, so here we have a ministry obviously related to the work of the oracle-givers in Psalms 110 and 132, but beginning:

> Give, O God, your judgements to the king
> and your right order to the royal one!
> May he judge your people with righteousness
> and your humble ones with justice!
> The mountains shall then bear prosperity for the people
> and the hills [rejoice] in the bounty of right order.

And so the minister continues to portray the ideal reign.

Comparison may be made also with Psalm 144, where the king's own prayer passes at verse 12 into a choral passage ('we'), very much in the style of creative words of blessing, and presumably chanted by a group with some prophetic affinity:

> So be[3] our sons like
>   plants well-grown when still young,
> our daughters like
>   columns carved for the building of a palace,
> our barns full of provisions of every kind,
> our flocks increasing by thousands
>   and ten thousands in our fields,
> our cattle heavy with young,
> bearing in due time without mishap,
> and no cry of pain in our courts.

Another example of speech to God passing into creative blessing for a reign is Psalm 21, where again the setting is probably the enthronement or renewal rites of the king in the autumn festival. The speaker who in verses 2–7/1–6 addresses Yahweh has the prophetic gift not only to approach God in intercession, but also to draw out the meaning of the preceding ceremonies with rich words which seem to bring the blessings nearer. Thus, all the while addressing God, he portrays the Davidic king as now resplendent with divine gifts, crowned by God himself, raised to everlasting life:

91

Yahweh, in your power the king is glad
and in your salvation how greatly he exults!
The desire of his heart you have given him
and the request of his lips you have not refused.
Truly you have met him with blessings of good,
you have placed on his head a crown of fine gold.
Life he asked of you and you have given it him,
length of days for ever and ever.
Great is his glory in your salvation,
splendour and majesty you have placed on him.
Truly you have appointed him blessings for ever,
you have gladdened him with joy in your presence.

In verses 9–13/8–12 the address probably turns to the Davidic
king and in the style of a blessing portrays the king's power over
all foes. Finally, verse 14/13, there is concluding invocation of
Yahweh, completing the circle of prayer and prophetic blessing.

Such prophetic blessings and intercessory wishes for the king
were obviously a particularly important part of the royal rites, to
judge from the quantity preserved. Thus there is also Psalm 20,
where the intercessory wish in verses 2–6/1–5 may be expressed
by a chorus (v. 6/5, 'we'); from some sign or inspiration an
individual then gains conviction to add confirmatory blessing
(vv. 7–9/6–8):

Now I know that Yahweh saves his anointed....

And again the circle is completed in prayer, which is of choral
form (v. 10/9):

O Yahweh, save the king!
May he answer us in the day when we cry!

Psalm 91[4] is best taken as a text of this kind. In the concluding
verses (14–16) God's speech is in the first person, while the rest of
the psalm is mostly in the form of authoritative promises or
blessings (God in third person), which equip the king with power
of protection, victory, glory, and enduring life. Psalm 121[5] is of
similar character. We can take it that when the king has expressed
trust in Yahweh (vv. 1–2), a prophetic minister answers with
Yahweh's assurances and blessings (God in third person), verse
3f.:

He will not allow your foot to stumble....
Yahweh will guard your going out and coming in
from now and until eternity.

Not least among such royal texts we must mention Psalm 45.[6]
The situation is the king's taking of another wife to add to his
collection. There are some indications that the ceremony was
joined to the others that concerned his office in the autumn
festival — in any case the wedding was conducted in the spirit of
those rites. The inspired seer has a few stern words of admonition
for the young lady, but for the most part he portrays the glory and
victory that God gives his king with the rich words of creative
blessing, finally aiming at the continuance of the dynasty through
children to be born. Of special interest is his introduction,
indicating the inspired excitement of a seer who is about to launch
such mighty phrases:

My heart seethes with favourable words
as I utter now my poem for the king,
my tongue darts like the pen of a skilled scribe.

The abundant prophetic materials in the royal psalms thus
show us prophetic ministers playing a key role in the fundamental
royal rites. They give direct oracles, or expound the divine will, or
pray to God for the king, or speak blessings and wishes over him.
In all these forms they use rich language, launching into the
world ideals of a righteous and compassionate society under a
ruler close in the counsels of God. It is not an exercise in word-
magic, trying to secure victory for one's own side regardless of
right and truth. It is an ideal which is said to be dependent on a
king's trust and commitment to God and on the degree to which
he can be the channel of God's own righteous rule. The task of
these prophetic ministers of psalmody was, in short, to use all the
strength of intercessory and creative words to foster a society
ruled and blessed by God.

Ritual and royal ideals in the prophets

When we turn to the prophetic collections, we find also many
passages projecting royal ideals and prophesying salvation which
God will bring through a Davidic ruler. These are closely related
to the psalmic texts in terms of the role ascribed to the Davidic

house. Can we then find here another link between the materials of the prophetic books and ceremonies of worship?

One might at first feel that there is a gulf between these two blocks of royal prophesyings, in that the psalms were spoken over current kings, while the prophetic corpus contains passages looking into the future for a king yet to come; the latter cases indeed may sometimes be post-exilic, when there was no king and no royal ceremonial. However, the psalm-texts are forward-looking in their own way; in Psalm 132, for example (p. 90), the view seems to stretch well down the dynastic avenue.[7] And texts in the prophets may sometimes arise from a contemporary royal event, while even in post-exilic times old forms and procedures may still be influential.

Let us examine the case of Isaiah 8.23b—9.6 (English 9.1b–7). There is an initial prediction that three areas of northern Israel incorporated into the Assyrian provinces in 734 and 732 b.c. will be restored:

> As in the former time [God] made contemptible
> the land of Zebulon and the land of Naphtali,
> so in the latter time he will make honoured
> the Coastal Route, East of the Jordan, and Galilee.

Then follows a poem in celebration of the royal event which has apparently given rise to this hopeful prediction. According to Alt, a Davidic king has been enthroned and thereby accepted by God as 'son'; as in Egyptian custom, God has also given him enthronement-names indicating the character of his forthcoming reign – an era of salvation. According to Wildberger, the event is rather that a prince has been born and invested as heir to the throne, a ceremony which would anticipate elements of an enthronement. In either case a religious ceremony is involved. Moreover, the form of 9.1–5/2–6 is that of communal thanksgiving addressed to God; acknowledgement is made that the suffering people have seen a great light and rejoice in new liberty, for he has decreed an end to foreign oppression and given a Davidic heir who will reign with salvation:

> People that were walking in darkness
> see a bright dawn,
> those who dwelt in the land of death's domain –
> on them the light shines!

You have given the nation new heart,[8]
you have given cause for great rejoicing.
They rejoice before you
with joy as of harvest-time,
with jubilation as when sharing spoils.

For the yoke that weighed on him [Israel]
and the yoke-bar on his back
and the rod of his driver
you have broken, as once you dealt with Midian.
Yes, all the boots of marchers that shook the ground
and the uniforms rolled in blood
shall be set ablaze and consumed by fire.

For a boy is born for us,
a son has been given to us
and power to rule has been laid on his back
and [God] has proclaimed his name:
HE WHO PLANS MARVELLOUSLY,
MIGHTY HERO,
FATHER FOR EVER,
BOUNTIFUL RULER.

This thanksgiving is rounded off with another predictive passage
(v. 6/7):

Increase of dominion and prosperity
shall be without end
over the throne of David and over his reign
to establish it and uphold it
with justice and right from now and for evermore –
the zeal of Yahweh of Hosts will achieve this.

The concluding affirmation that Yahweh is determined to achieve
the aforesaid salvation through his king, equivalent to such
prophetic conclusions as 'for the mouth of Yahweh has spoken
it', 'utterance of Yahweh', etc., can be matched by culminating
affirmations in psalms which I take to be from the visionary royal
rituals;[9] thus Psalm 22.32/31:

To a people yet to be born they shall say,
He has achieved it!

Or Psalm 118.23–4:

From Yahweh's presence this marvel has come....
Now, this day, Yahweh has achieved it.

But throughout Isaiah 9.1–6/2–7 there are so many resemblances to traditional Israelite and Egyptian[10] royal language, that it seems to be an example[11] of the utterances which would commonly accompany the sacred investitures. The elements of prediction in this text belong naturally to the circumstances and only go much beyond the forward-looking hopes and blessings of the psalms in the particularizing statement preceding the main poem.

In the early post-exilic period Zechariah is an example of a prophet who would be associated with the enthronement of a new king, if it were to happen. For he recounts his commission from God to perform an anticipatory sign, which includes designation of God's chosen ruler, indication of his destined task, and the preparing, bestowing, and preservation of the crown (Zech. 6.9–14). This then reflects a kind of prophetic ministry which contributed specific application at the installations, pointing to the particular man and the particular destiny:

See, a man whose name is The Sprout
and from under him life will sprout
and he will build the temple of Yahweh.

Yes, he it is who will build the temple of Yahweh
and he will receive majesty
and shall sit and rule on his throne
and a priest shall be [beside him] on his throne
and they shall be in full accord.

A contemporary prophet of similar role at an enthronement would be Haggai, for he had already come forward with an oracle to indicate the relevant turn of events, the particular man chosen by God, and the destiny of this man as God's seal of authority (2.20–23):

And the word of Yahweh came to Haggai....

Say to Zerubbabel, governor of Judah:
I am shaking the heavens and the earth
and will overturn the throne of kingdoms
and destroy the strength of the kingdoms of the nations
and overturn chariots and riders
and horses and riders shall fall each to the sword of his fellow.

On that day – utterance of Yahweh of Hosts –
I will take you Zerubbabel, son of Shealtiel,

my servant – utterance of Yahweh –
and I will make you like my signet ring
for I have chosen you,
– utterance of Yahweh of Hosts.

The richest material, however, comes from within the period
of the Exile, from Isaiah 40—55. We have already noted
something of the 'festal' character of these prophecies (p. 27), the
themes of Yahweh's triumph, advent, and new reign of salvation
being applied to the current political situation. But it seems that
this prophetic tradition had been concerned not only with the
projection of Yahweh's festal triumph but also with the tasks of
designating Yahweh's king and pronouncing his destiny. The
clearest evidence of this is Isaiah 42. First an oracle is delivered in
which God designates the royal leader:

See, my servant whom I uphold,
my chosen one in whom my soul delights!

Then the divine word confers charisma and destiny:

I put my spirit on him,
he shall radiate good rule to the nations,
he will not shout nor raise
nor make loud his voice in the streets,
the trodden reed he will not break off,
the failing wick he will not put out –
truly he will radiate good rule.
Nor will he fail nor be broken off
until he establishes good rule on earth
and for his rule far coastlands wait.

Next the prophet delivers an oracle directly to the chosen one.
The legitimacy of the new ruler and the nature of his task are
further emphasized, but especially the fact that all is of God
(42.5):

Thus says the god Yahweh –
creator of the heavens, stretching them out,
craftsman of the earth and all she bears,
bestower of breath on all her population,
of spirit on all that walk on her –

I am Yahweh,
I have summoned you as the rightful heir,
your hand I grasp,
I fashion you and appoint you
as a covenant of promise for peoples,
as a light for nations.
You will open up the eyes of the blind,
you will bring out the prisoners from the dungeon,
dwellers in darkness from the prison.

I am Yahweh,
that is my name
and my glory I will not yield to another
nor my splendour to idols.
The former things – see, they have been fulfilled,
new things now I declare,
before they sprout I inform you.

The continuation is again thoroughly in the festal tradition, being psalmic acclamation of Yahweh's new era of kingship and triumph and salvation (42.10f.):

Sing to Yahweh a song ever new,
his praise from the end of the earth.... (p. 28)

The resemblance to the psalms may throw light on the most puzzling feature of these chapters – that the designated servant is not clearly identified, as he is in Haggai and Zechariah. Here, rather, is a tradition of prophetic ministry which, like that of the psalmic prophets, works with liturgical formulations that soar mysteriously on high, not bound to specific identifications. The few allusions to Cyrus, to leaving Babylon and returning to Zion are but meagre indications of the historical circumstances. For the most part these chapters move on the mysterious plane of the psalmic seers.

It would be inevitably controversial to press the argument further through detailed treatment of the other servant songs.[12] But, weighty as they are, they cannot be altogether passed over. I consider these also to be in the style and tradition of the royal rites. The mysterious quality remains but is partially resolved in Isaiah 55. This culminating chapter can most directly be taken to bring the designating and destiny-unfolding servant songs into relation with the irrevocable covenant to the house of David[13] (55.3f.):

Incline your ear and come to me,
hear and a good life shall be yours
for I will make with you an eternal covenant,
the irrevocable promises to David....

In these last three songs there is increasing use of the theme of
apparent failure and suffering, and my view is that the prophecies
are using elements of ordeal and humiliation from the old festal
drama of royal initiation or renewal, and thinking of them in
relation to the blows that had fallen on David's line. The
accompanying theme of hope and eventual triumph (again from
the old rites) is thought of in relation to the future role of David's
line in the prophesied era of salvation. On this view of the songs
the prophetic contribution to the dramatic nature of the old royal
rites must have been all the more extensive. For it would then
appear that the prophetic voice might express words not only of
God, prophet, or congregation, but also of the king[14] – hence the
presentation of the servant's words in the first person in the
second and third songs (chs. 49 and 50). Further, the ministry
might be exercised by a group, a chorus, so that in the fourth song
(52.13—53.12) the central section (53.1–10), lying between two
speeches of God, is uttered by such a prophetic group, unfolding
the secret of the servant which has been revealed to them. We
may compare a related scene in Psalm 118 where a group
likewise contributes an interpretation of the royal suffering
(v. 22f.):

The stone which the builders rejected
has become the chief cornerstone.
From Yahweh's presence this marvel has come,
it is most wonderful to our eyes.
Now, this day, Yahweh has achieved it,
let us celebrate and rejoice over it....

The prophetic chorus in Isaiah 53 likewise has a story of rejection
and exaltation to unfold. Here it is,[15] set between the
accompanying direct oracles (52.13f.):

See, my servant shall be triumphant,
he will be very high, exalted, supreme!
As many were dumbfounded at [him],
so I have anointed his person above men
and his form above mankind,

so he shall asperge many nations,
kings shall shut their mouths before him
for things never told they see
and things unheard of they contemplate.

Who believes our revelation,
to whom is the working of Yahweh disclosed?

Now he came up like a shoot before him
and like a slip from arid ground.
He had no beauty, no majesty.
When we saw him there was no feature to admire.
He was scorned and avoided by people,
a tormented man, familiar with disease.

But ours were the diseases he bore,
ours were the torments he carried.
In our ignorance we deemed him plagued
and smitten by God and punished,
but for our sins he was pierced
and for our misdeeds he was crushed,
chastisement fell on him for our healing
and through his wounds we became whole.

We had all strayed like a flock,
we had each gone our own way
and Yahweh brought down on him
the guilt that was ours.
He was driven and afflicted
but he did not open his mouth,
like a lamb to the slaughter he was led
and like a sheep silent under the shearers
he did not open his mouth.

Of power and rule he was deprived
and who gave heed to his rank?
He was severed from the land of the living,
for the sin of my people he was stricken.
[God] appointed his grave with the wicked,
his burial mound with the worthless
although he had done no violence
and there was no wrong in his mouth.
But Yahweh willed to crush him with sufferings –
truly his soul made an offering for sin!
Now he shall see descendants, he shall live long
and through his rule the will of Yahweh shall flourish.

100

The outcome of his soul's pain he shall see
and be satisfied.
By his humiliation the righteous one makes right,
yes, my servant [rights] the multitudes
for it is their guilt he has borne.

Therefore I give the multitudes as his portion
and the masses he may take as his spoil
in reward for exposing his soul to death
and interposing himself for sinners.

We may consider one further example of prophecy arising
from the royal rites, Zechariah 9.9–10. This small but striking
piece is preserved in one of the latest collections but in itself
accords closely with texts of the pre-exilic autumn festival. The
prophet calls upon Zion in hymnic style to give triumphant
acclaim as her king makes ceremonial entry. A similar festal call
and announcement is well represented elsewhere with reference
to the entry of God as King (cf. Zeph. 3.14; Isa. 40.9–11;
Pss. 48.11; 97.8; 147.12–13), but in the present case attention is
focused on his Davidic servant:

Rejoice greatly, fair Zion,
Shout the triumph-cries, Damsel Jerusalem!
See, your king comes to you....

The prophet had then to draw out the significance of the physical
rite, indeed to give it its proper meaning with creative words. So
he declares that the king comes to begin a reign characterized by
justice and peace and world-wide extent. This characterization
begins with pregnant words:

See, your king comes to you,
he who is righteous and bearing salvation,
humble, and riding on a donkey,
on a young ass pure of breed.

The allusions to righteousness, salvation, and humility may imply
in the first place that the king comes from rites in which these
attributes have been proved and manifested. The ritual of royal
installation or renewal seems to have stressed the need for the
king to show humility and faith, passing through symbolic
sufferings before being finally accepted by Yahweh, raised to
salvation and glory. Then came his triumphant procession up to

Zion, as is best illustrated by Psalm 118. This tells of the rite in words that often chime in with our Zechariah text: the leader 'comes' or 'enters' (Ps. 118.19, 20, 26) through the gates symbolic of 'righteousness' (vv. 19, 20); God has raised him from suffering to 'salvation' (vv. 15, 21, 25); 'rejoicing' (v. 24) and 'triumph-cries' (v. 15) ring forth. That Zechariah's king rides a young and pure-bred donkey no doubt accords with royal tradition (cf. Gen. 49.11), and may, in contrast to the war-horse (Zech. 9.10), symbolize peace; but the New Testament may preserve a further point – the rite of the new era required an animal hitherto unridden (Mark 11.2).

The Hebrew text continues with 'And I will destroy', thus giving the passage direct oracular form, while the Greek, preferred by some scholars, has 'and he will destroy' – the prophet in this case having authority himself to unfold the destiny bestowed by God (Zech. 9.10):

> And he will destroy the chariot from Ephraim
> and the war-horse from Jerusalem
> and the war-bow shall be destroyed
> and he will decree peace for the nations.

This is in accord with the old liturgical ideal well represented by Psalm 46.9–10/8–9, where Yahweh's festal triumph includes the destruction of bows, spears, and vehicles. The Zechariah text ends on the theme of world-wide rule and in language very similar to that of the royal blessing-prayer, Psalm 72.8 (p. 91); thus Zechariah:

> And his rule will stretch from sea to sea
> and from the river to the ends of the earth.

Thus Zechariah 9.9–10 gives us further insight into the co-operation of prophets in festal rites. In a style very similar to the psalmic texts, a prophet might further convey God's mind regarding a royal initiation or renewal. Just as the advent of God required interpretation for weal or woe (pp. 32, 39), so the significant moments in the Davidic ruler's rites called for declarations of the divine mind. The Zechariah text is evidence of such a prophetic ministry, here able to give a good message. And it is notable that the style, devoid of any historical particularity, is of a piece with that of the royal psalms.

In our review of the texts, then, we have seen that prophetic ministries assisted in the greatest moments of the royal rites, reaching far into the profoundest mysteries of life and faith, and conveying their insights in dramatic forms of great potency. So committed were the circles concerned in this ministry, that even in the disruption of the Exile they expressed their hopes in their traditional manner.

We have seen that prophets of the type whose words are found in the Books of Isaiah, Haggai, and Zechariah took part in the ceremonies of royal initiation or renewal. They might relate the ideals to the current situation, delivering oracles designating a particular person and characterizing his task and giving him grace. Often, however, they remain close to the prophetic ministry exemplified in the royal psalms, in that their utterances are traditional and timeless, not expressed in terms of an identifiable person or situation.

The examples in the prophetic books rival the psalms in poetic power, dramatic form, and vision of inexhaustible significance. In times of greatest suffering and despair they sent out shafts of light and inspired men with unquenchable hope. They told of God's order of salvation that would be sent with the man of his choice. Through the house of David God would achieve expiation and reconciliation, a just society where the weak are not oppressed, a world where all species rejoice in harmony and love.

I hear many of their very words still sounding through the world, most movingly perhaps in the inspired music of Handel's *Messiah*. And ever and again I know that these were among the greatest and truest poets ever given to the world.

5   Concluding remarks

We began by studying a high point of Israelite worship, the festal advent of Yahweh. The psalms showed well this climax in the actualization of his defeat of chaos and his new reign as saviour in Zion. The relevant psalms themselves had prophetic quality, as, for example, in their visions of Yahweh's coming and indications that the ceremonies waited upon pronouncements of his will.

We found that this liturgical experience was continued and given current application in materials preserved in the prophets, such as Habakkuk 3, Nahum, Jeremiah 46—51, and several parts of the Isaiah collection. The defeat of chaos became that of Assyria, Egypt, Babylon, etc. We saw such prophets serving in the festival to interpret its message and authorize its gospel, as appropriate. Their eloquent and visionary poetry was a direct contribution to the sacramental liturgy, for in their potent words and imaginative pictures the reality of the divine order began to take shape.

In some examples of their work – Zephaniah and Amos – the coming of Yahweh is seen as especially dangerous to Israel. This did not mean the birth of a different species of prophecy. It is simply that in a particular situation the spotlight shifts to aspects of Israelite life that would not be able to endure the coming of God. It was especially when a prophet gave such warnings that reference was made to a greater advent, the day of Yahweh, still to come, but leaving little time for repentance. Of this day of Yahweh the festival was a kind of sacramental anticipation. It could be, as later tradition has it, that these same warning prophets went on to envisage the joyful restoration of the penitent remnant.

It was the psalms which gave us the most rounded examples of the speeches Yahweh would make when his manifestation before his worshipping people was signified and acknowledged. But there was much similar oracular address to Israel in the prophets, our examples being from Isaiah, Micah, Amos, and Deutero-Isaiah. Here then, in psalms and prophets, were deposits of a ministry which articulated the mind of Yahweh when he periodically renewed his bond with his covenanters and exhorted them to walk in his ways. A stern and threatening tone is characteristic of these speeches, and it is consistent that occasionally this ministry would go to the extreme and pronounce the worshippers to be at present unacceptable to Yahweh.

Wonderful as is the religion of the God Who Speaks, still more wonderful is that of the God Who Converses, answering his worshippers' calls of distress and laments, arguing and pleading with them. The correlation of lament and oracular answer was found to be attested in the psalms, with indications that the setting was often a great occasion of worship – festival or specially decreed rites of supplication. Beseeching God, no less than bringing back his answer, was a charismatic task, and similar material in the prophets indicated that the same person could fulfil both tasks (as indeed the histories show also in the case of Samuel, Elijah, etc.). Habakkuk was a clear example, but Jeremiah too seems to have engaged in this double task – his cross was that for all the earnestness with which he sought to move Yahweh to relent, he still had to report an ever harder reply. In Joel and Hosea, however, we found examples of intercessors who were able at last to change their oracles of doom to words of acceptance. The God Who Converses was in evidence also in the lamenting assemblies of the Exile. After years of doubt or silence, clear answers of hope came through Ezekiel and Deutero-Isaiah. Although the supplicatory side is preserved only in brief allusions, Deutero-Isaiah is really a splendid flowering of the dialogue tradition; Yahweh gives resounding answers and eloquent arguments, 'speaking to the heart' of his complaining people.

A particularly significant bond between psalms and prophets was found in the visions of Davidic rule. The basic situation here for both collections was the worship where the Davidic office was consecrated and prayed over. Such dedications of a particular ruler were the opportunity for prophets to present the noblest ideals of society ruled according to God's will. Thus in the royal psalms, the messianic prophecies, and the servant songs, we meet many of the greatest visions born in worship.

At the end of our little journey together through these great poems, what can we say in general of Israelite worship and prophecy? We have seen more clearly that the great occasions of Israelite worship were experienced as meetings with God, and, moreover, with God active in his fundamental work of judgement and salvation. With visionary and hence 'prophetic' power the psalms convey awareness of his advent and are joined in this task by the prophets. Prophecy thus does not seem to be a separate movement breaking in upon the liturgy, but rather to grow from within it. The liturgy had always had the service of prophetic ministries to authorize its proceedings and interpret its message. Prophets and psalmists unite in carrying out these tasks and vivifying the liturgical scenes. The psalms primarily give the regular liturgical framework, the prophets the particular, occasional interpretation, but the distinction is far from absolute.

Of the greatest interest is the development of divine speech and also of debate between God and people. In the intense solemnity of encounter with the divine, searching judgements about the morals of the society were expressed and inculcated; human need was passionately voiced, insights into the divine fidelity were won through long wrestling in prayer. We may say then that worship in Israel was characterized by the word, above all the poetic word; flying on great wings of imagination, it bore thought and feeling from God to man and from man to God, making a true communion of mind and soul.

The vision, then, that illumined Israelite worship was primarily grasped and shared through rapturous poetry, however much it was supported by music, dancing, and drama. While the prophets served to link the vision with contemporary events, they united also with the psalmists in maintaining the eschatological dimension of the liturgy. Especially in the rites of kingship, they shared in the ideals of the perfect society and in that present joy which arises where worship transcends time and through present contact with God sees already the completion of his work. Here worship attains its goal, as the realities of this fleeting world are outshone by the greater reality. Worship itself has become vision.

Notes

INTRODUCTION

1 Cf. his *Einleitung*, pp. 329–80 and his 'Jesaia 33'.

2 *Psalmenstudien* III and *Psalms in Israel's Worship*, ch. 12.

3 *CPAI* and now *CPIP*. For the other authors, see the Bibliography. A survey of passages in the prophets which have been called 'liturgies' is given by Gerlach. He notes the approaches of various commentators and considers the broad effect of such passages in the prophets' message.

CHAPTER 1
GOD'S ADVENT IN VICTORY AND SALVATION

1 See *FDDI*, ch. 2 and *TI*, p. 263f.

2 For this force of *nōrā* see my 'Some misunderstood Hebrew words'. Cf. New English Bible on Zeph. 2.11, 'appear with all his terrors'.

3 *maśkil*, cf. Jer. 23.5; Isa. 52.13. On this translation the object of the four-times repeated verb *zmr* remains constant.

4 Assuming *'rbwt* is equivalent to Ugaritic *'rpt*. Otherwise, 'rides over the deserts', as *SKAI*, p. 78.

5 Cf. *SKAI*, p. 88.

6 See *FDDI*, esp. pp. 38–41.

7 'You' feminine, either for an office-holder or (collectively) of the prophetesses (Ps. 68.12/11). Or there may be a personification, 'tidings-bearer Zion', *FDDI*, p. 38.

8 Cf. my detailed treatment in *ZAW* (1964).

9 So also over Pss. 17; 86; 90.

10 As over Ps. 7.

11 So my *ONHZ*.

12 See p. 69; ch. 3, note 1.

13 The line is literally 'and there is the covert of his power'. Cf. Job 36.32.

14 For this good sense without emendation, see my 'Origin and meaning'.

15 The depiction could be taken literally after a year of drought, or impressionistically of the usual effect of the long summer drought (cf. the Tammuz laments, my 'Origin and meaning', p. 162).

16 Cf. *ONHZ*; *RBH* II.

17 *ḥuṣṣab* as Hophal of a root *ṣbb* (Arabic 'wash away') or *nṣb* (Akkadian 'suck out'). Otherwise, *ḥaṣṣab*, 'The image (is made captive....)'. See *RBH* II with references to *JTS* (1964), p. 296f.; (1969), p. 220f., etc.

18 Cf. BDB, p. 851, *ṣīṣ* and p. 661, *nṣ'* (dubious).

19 Or 'inhabitants of Moab'.

20 Cf. Pritchard, p. 131.

21 von Waldow; Westermann, p. 25 (English p. 27); cf. Whybray, pp. 29–30.

22 *FDDI*, p. 15.

23 Rather than 'from Edom', see *BHS*.

24 Assuming a noun *boṣrā* (formed like *šomrā*). Otherwise, 'than of a woman harvesting grapes' *(bōṣᵉrā)*.

25 Cf. my treatment in *ONHZ* and *RBH* I.

26 Cf. note 2 above.

27 Cf. p. 3f,

28 Cf. p. 21; *KP*, pp. 98–9; *RBH* I, p. 89.

29 E.g., Ekron (*'eqrōn*), 'to be uprooted' (*'qr*). Several other roots seem to be played on: *ḥbl, kn', krt, grš, šdd*; see *RBH* I, p. 89f.

30 Cf. Pss. 85 and 126; Mowinckel, *Psalms in Israel's Worship* I, p. 146; *RBH* I, 90–1.

31 *RBH* I, p. 93.

32 *RBH* I, p. 96.

33 *RBH* I, p. 96.

34 Alignment of Amos with the recognized prophets is expressed in 2.12; 3.7–8; 7.15. His mastery of tradition, his fine style and association with the *nōqᵉdīm* of Tekoa (1.1) may indicate that he came from temple circles and had care of temple flocks and lands. Even if the most markedly liturgical passages in Amos stem from later tradition, it is still significant that the tradition comes down through temple circles. The King James Version's understanding of 7.14–15 follows that of the earliest Version, the Greek.

35 It can be argued that the oracles against Tyre, Edom, and Judah have been added in later tradition. Without the Tyre oracle the north-west angle in the pattern would be unrepresented. The remaining material, amply covering north and south, would still be related to the fuller pattern, a pattern which tradition would then have aptly restored.

36 Cf. also Amos' uses of *'ōsīp* in 7.8; 8.2.

CHAPTER 2
GOD'S ADDRESS TO HIS COVENANTED PEOPLE

1 I take *b-* as a Beth Essentiae and imagine that the special fanfares that mark

new and full moon of the new year are sounded together for this most solemn moment.

2   'For' as in parallel line. He has committed himself to the observance and thus promised to meet his covenant-partner.

3   *'al* as 'from over', see Dahood; 'against' is possible. Lev. 23.33f. links the appointment of the autumn festival with the Exodus.

4   Cf. *lqḥ* in 1 Sam. 12.3f.

5   See Wildberger.

6   'Your' is implied by the context, cf. v. 11a.

7   See Würthwein, 'Kultpolemik'.

8   Perhaps from 'Zion' as mother, *FDDI*, p. 19f.

9   A similar didactic use of this form is found in the processional psalm 24 and in Isa. 33 (p. 63).

10 Cf. Engnell. For a somewhat different approach cf. Keel, who has examined the vision with comparison of divine beings depicted on seals, etc.

11 See *KP*, pp. 87–96.

12 Cf. Kaiser, Wildberger, and *RBH* II.

13 It was the 'best man's' duty not only to lead in the festive celebrations, but also to represent the bridegroom if, during the period of the engagement, there was cause for dispute or complaint.

14 Cf. *FDDI*, p. 19f. It is obviously a question of Yahweh's 'marriage' rather than his long-standing relation to Israel-Zion, and hence the festal setting, where the fundamentals of society and religion are enacted as new, is appropriate.

CHAPTER 3
DIALOGUE OF GOD AND CONGREGATION

1   For prophets as intercessors, see in general Gen. 20.7; Exod. 8.4/8; 32.11f; Num. 14.13f; Deut. 9.18, 25; 1 Sam. 7.5f; 12.9; 15.11; 1 Kings 17.20–4; 18.36f; 2 Kings 19.2f; Jer. 4.9–10; 15.1; 42.2f; Amos 7.1–6.

2   Another view is that a previously given oracle is here cited back to God as part of the lament (cf. *CPIP*, pp. 170–2). But note the examples that I further cite of oracles given as fresh responses, and followed by reaction of worshippers.

3   Cf. D. W. Thomas on Ps. 13.2.

4   Or 'you were to rule'. For this use of the imperative cf. Obad. 12–14 of deeds already done.

5   Cf. 2 Sam. 19.29. Or 'I took you to be gods'.

6   So S.T.V. M, 'their arm'.

7   Cf. *BHS*.

8   Cf. Fohrer, vol. 3, p. 246; Whybray, p. 256.

9   With a few manuscripts, cf. *BHS*.

10   Or, perhaps, 'shall be exiled into a land they do not know' (Reventlow).

11   Verse 4 may contain 'Deuteronomic' expansion, though Reventlow argues against this.

12   Added to suggest the effect of the verb 'Lament' in feminine singular.

13   Prophets, cf. Isa. 21.6; Jer. 6.17; Ezek. 33.7; Hab. 2.1, and above, p. 60.

14   M, 'you' masculine can be revocalized as feminine, *BHS*.

15   *ṭrp, hlk, šūb, šḥr, rp'*.

16   So G.

17   See *FDDI*, p. 42.

18   Cf. Ps. 22; Westermann; *FDDI*, p. 46.

19   Cf. Westermann; *FDDI*, p. 67.

CHAPTER 4
VISIONS OF DAVIDIC RULE

1   See *KP*, ch. 3.

2   See KP, p. 209, n. 25.

3   *'ªšer*, cf. BDB, p. 83, 8b.

4   *KP*, pp. 57–8.

5   *KP*, p. 83.

6   *KP*, pp. 118–20.

7   Cf. also the end of Ps. 22; *KP*, pp. 36, 167.

8   Lit., 'you have made the nation great to itself'.

9   For Pss. 22 and 118, see *KP*, pp. 34, 61.

10   See parallels in Wildberger.

11   Rather than draw this simple conclusion, Wildberger (p. 108) states (my translation): 'One may accordingly venture the conclusion that 9.5f. is to be understood as prophetic *imitation of a proclamation* of the court at Jerusalem which used to follow soon after the birth of a royal child on the occasion of his induction into the dignity of crown prince.'

12   42.1–4 or 1–7; 49.1–6 or 1–9; 50.4–9 or 4–11; 52.13—53.12; my view is set out in *FDDI*.

13   The view that the covenant is here abrogated in its original royal sense and instead applied to the nation is, I believe, read into the chapter by scholars who have misunderstood the preceding chapters; see *FDDI*, pp. 87–9.

14   Cf. Exod. 4.16; 7.1. Johnson in *CPIP* argues that psalms were composed and sung on behalf of the king and others by cultic prophets.

15   For questions of translation, see *FDDI*, pp. 75–84.

Bibliography

Alt, A., 'Jesaja 8.23—9.6', in *Kleine Schriften* II (Munich 1953), pp. 206–25.

Dahood, M., *Psalms*, Anchor Bible series, 3 vols. New York 1966–70.

Eaton, J. H., *Obadiah, Nahum, Habakkuk, Zephaniah*. London 1961.

— 'The origin and meaning of Hab. 3', *ZAW*, 76 (1964), pp. 144–71.

— 'Some misunderstood words for God's self-revelation', *The Bible Translator*, 25 (1974), pp. 331–8.

— *Kingship and the Psalms*. London 1976.

— (ed.), *Readings in Biblical Hebrew*, 2 vols., 1976–8, available direct from Department of Theology, University of Birmingham, Birmingham B15 2TT.

— *Festal Drama in Deutero-Isaiah*. London 1979.

— 'The Psalms and Israelite Worship', in *Tradition and Interpretation*, ed. G. W. Anderson (Oxford 1979), pp. 238–73.

Engnell, I., *The Call of Isaiah*. Uppsala Universitets Årsskrift 1949:4.

Fohrer, G., *Das Buch Jesaja*, 3 vols. Zürich/Stuttgart 1964–7.

Gerlach, M., *Die prophetischen Liturgien des Alten Testaments*, dissertation. Bonn 1967.

Gunkel, H., 'Jesaia 33, eine prophetische Liturgie', *ZAW*, 42 (1924), pp. 177–208.

— *Einleitung in die Psalmen*, completed by J. Begrich. Göttingen 1933.

Humbert, P., *Problèmes du livre d'Habacuc*. Mémoires de l'Univ. de Neuchâtel 18. 1944.

Johnson, A. R., *The Cultic Prophet in Ancient Israel*. Cardiff (1944), 2nd edn 1962.

— *Sacral Kingship in Ancient Israel*. Cardiff (1955), 2nd edn 1967.

— *The Cultic Prophet and Israel's Psalmody*. Cardiff 1979.

Kaiser, O., *Isaiah 1—12*. The Old Testament Library (from German edn of 1963). London 1972.

Keel, O., *Jahwe-Visionen und Siegelkunst*, Stuttgarter Bibelstudien 84/5. Stuttgart 1977.

Mowinckel, S., *Psalmenstudien I–VI*. Kristiania 1921–4, reproduced Amsterdam 1961.

— *The Psalms in Israel's Worship*, 2 vols. Oxford 1962.

Pritchard, J. B. (ed.), *Ancient Near Eastern Texts*, 2nd edn. Princeton 1955.

Reventlow, H. Graf, *Liturgie und prophetisches Ich bei Jeremia*. Gütersloh 1963.

111

BIBLIOGRAPHY

Thomas, D. Winton, *The Text of the Revised Psalter.* London 1963.
Waldow, H. E. von, 'The message of Deutero-Isaiah', *Interpretation*, 22 (1968), pp. 259–87. This gathers up elements from the following two works:
— *Anlass und Hintergrund der Verkündigung des Deuterojesaja*, dissertation. Bonn 1953.
— *Der traditionsgeschichtliche Hintergrund der prophetischen Gerichtsreden, Beihefte zur ZAW*, 85. Berlin 1963.
Westermann, C., *Das Buch Jesaja Kap. 40—66.* Göttingen 1966 (translated as *Isaiah 40—66*, London 1969).
— 'Jes. 48 und die Bezeugung gegen Israel', in *Festschrift Vriezen* (Wageningen 1966), pp. 356–66.
Whybray, R. N., *Isaiah 40—66.* New Century Bible. London 1975.
Wildberger, H., *Jesaja.* Biblischer Kommentar Altes Testament X.1. Neukirchen-Vluyn 1965–.
Würthwein, E., 'Die Ursprung der prophetischen Gerichtsrede', *Zeitschrift für Theologie und Kirche*, 49 (1952), pp. 1–15.
— 'Kultpolemik oder Kultbescheid?' in *Tradition und Situation* (Weiser Festschrift), ed. E. Würthwein and O. Kaiser (Göttingen 1963), pp. 115–31.

Index of Subjects

Index of Biblical References